AF490724

CONTAINER GARDENING FOR BEGINNERS

A beginner's guide for growing plants, herbs, fruits and vegetables in pots, tubes and other containers. How to create your perfect garden safely.

CHAPTER ONE

Hydroponic Cropping

Upon initial commercial implementation of hydroponics, only three crop species were widely grown: tomato, basil, and lettuce. A large variety of crops (i.e., cucumber, pepper, strawberry, roses, and potatoes) are successfully grown hydroponically today. Even so, most commercially available hydroponic systems are still based on either tomato or herbal and lettuce growing requirements. The author visited a hydroponic greenhouse in the early 1970s where the grower successfully moved from growing tomatoes to chrysanthemum flower production in a gravel-sump ebb-and-flow method (sometimes referred to as flood-and-drain) using the same procedures as those for tomatoes. It indicated to me that many different plant types could be successfully grown hydroponically, although the chosen hydroponic system was not planned specifically for that crop. This continues to be proved true after the initial encounter. Today, using mainly two nutrient solution distribution methods, ebb-and-flow and drip irrigation, a wide variety of fruits, flowers, and even tree crops are cultivated hydroponically. The only exceptions will be for herbs and lettuce, where the Nutrient Film Technique (NFT) approach is favored (Christian, 1997, 1999; Furukawa, 2000; Morgan, 2000b; Alexander, 2001a; Smith, 2002c); and some lettuce growers do use the raft system (Morgan, 2002f; Spillane, 2001).

On view at the Kraft Show in the Disney EPCOT Center, Orlando, Florida, an outstanding example of what is possible hydroponically can be seen (Ricks 1996). Visitors who take the boat ride through the show can see several different crop plants developing in various hydroponic setups. Another fascinating application of hydroponics is at the Hydroponicum, located on the west coast of Scotland (Savage, 1995;

Farquhar, 2003). A closer look at these rising systems, and what experiments are being performed but not on show, can be seen if the visitor takes the "behind the scenes tour." In three dif-ferent climatic regimes within the Hydroponicum a variety of temperate to tropical plants are being grown hydroponically. Many of the plants are grown in a specially built Pyramid Pot in which a passive Wick System provides the nutrient solution, both created by the Hydroponicum founder Robert Irvine (Savage, 1995).

For the most part, hydroponics and growth are associated in an environmentally regulated setting, such as a greenhouse, as hydroponics is usually not considered a method of growth in the open (outdoor) world. Nevertheless, it is important to note that open-environment hydroponic systems were commonly used during the Second World War, when vegetables were hydroponically grown to provide fresh produce for troops serving in the Pacific camp areas. Following WWII in 1950, the author visited a number of hydroponic farms in southern Florida; in ebb-and-flow gravel beds, the crop cultivated was tomato. Some of the early hydroponics literature in the 1950s and '60s.

Today, much of the existing hydroponics literature addresses this problem as a type of "Regulated Agriculture Environment (CEA)." Hence, much of the success associated with hydroponics may have more to do with advancements in environmental management than those associated with the hydroponic system used. One wonders if the future of hydroponics as a major crop production system lies in settings other than open field, as it was in its initial years of use.

Hydroponic growing systems differ in size, operating characteristics and reliability, and are typically more costly and operationally complex than most other growing methods. High value cash crops (such as tomatoes) or specialty crops (such as herbs) are therefore more frequently selected for hydroponic production than lower cash value crops. While initial costs may be high, hydroponics as a crop production method can be highly profitable. Several of the major drawbacks of hydroponics are the high cost of capital for most widely used growing systems, regular incidences of root disease, and possible insufficiencies of nutrient elements. However, these issues are being tackled and strides are being made to solve the cost problems and insufficiencies associated with the hydroponic growing process.

It should be recalled that hydroponics is not a good panacea, irrespective of what crop is being grown or what growing method is being employed. For general, even if a hydroponic growing technique is used, the cultural requirements for a crop do not change. In certain cases, greater ability on the grower's part may be needed to be effective when using a hydroponic system.

Hydroponics will not invalidate the plants' genetic character; plant growth and fruit production do not surpass what is genetically feasible regardless of the growing method employed.

Hydroponics provides the ability to monitor the water supply and the vital elements to plant roots, thereby ensuring a continuous optimum supply, which in turn will boost plant efficiency. Greenhouse-raised crops such as tomato, cucumber, pepper, and lettuce may be cultivated over a longer period of time than is feasible for the cultivation of land. Hence yield comparisons may be misleading for that hydroponically grown versus grown-grown soil, for yields are likely identical if compared equally.

For example, hydroponic development may be the only choice when growing conditions are such that no other growing method is suitable due to poor soil conditions and extreme climatic regions, and for growing in outer space and roof-top gardening (Wilson, 2002a).

The growing interest of the public in wanting to purchase "organically produced" produce can have a huge effect on the future of hydroponics (Parker, 1989; Morgan, 1997c; Landers, 2001). Being only pesticide / herbicide-free is no longer the only aspect that draws environmentally friendly customers who are searching for "organically grown" food items. Schoenstein (2001) notes that "in addition to organic, environmentally-controlled, green-house agriculture enables farmers to enter more niche markets because of their ability to expand a crop to a much longer seas With the increase in North America's massive, large-scale greenhouses, the value of conventional off-season output is declining while the demand for organic crops remains high. "The change from inorganic to organic hydroponics will involve the creation of suitable growing media and formulations of nutrient solutions that qualify as organic.

Schoenstein (2001) describes a greenhouse operation which uses an organic NFT growing system to produce lettuce and herbs.

Progressive Developments

The original hydroponic growing system was the form of standing aerated nutrient solution, a process considered unsuitable for commercial use. However, Cunningham (1997) explains the use of this technique (which he defines as the modified Gericke method for growing green bean, tomato and zucchini squash, a device that does not need electrical power and is fairly easy to use. Kratky (1996) explains the general principles and concepts of a non-circulating growing method for hydroponic growing lettuce, tomato,

Wilcox (1983) published a detailed analysis of those hydroponic systems currently in use around the world, water or solution culture, sand culture, aggregate culture, and nutrient film style at that time. The ebb-and-flow process (Fischer et al., 1990) was the original hydroponic growing technique for commercial applications and was closely followed by the gravity flow bed technique. Many methods have different uses, such as the lettuce raft system (Spillane, 2001; Morgan, 2002f) and the aeroponics (Nichols, 2002; Wilson, 2002b).

In 1979, Cooper's (1979b) developed the Nutrient Film Technique (NFT) was hailed as a groundbreaking move forward that would alter the hydroponic growing process for all crops. Yet this hasn't proven true (see pages). However, Smith (2000) mentions many places where the NFT approach is used for tomato growing (Christian 1999), strawberry, and pepper growing. Smith (2001e) offers guidance on the use of this method for tomato growing. Today, both the NFT method (Alexander, 2001; Smith, 2002c, d) and deep water NFT (Jones,

1990) are mainly used for the processing of lettuce and herbs in hydroponic form. Morgan (I999c) defines the various gullies and channels designs for use in NFT applications. Smith (2004) also offers guidance for designing and producing NFT gullies.

With the implementation of drip irrigation at a particular point and precise amount, water and/or a nutrient solution could be dispensed. Using this method, growers can grow hydroponically in inert media containers, such as perlite (Day, 1991) in bags (Bauerle, 1984) or BATO buckets or blocks and slabs of rockwool (Smith, 1987; Sonneveld, 1989; Van Patten, 1989, 1991; Johnson, 2001a). Today this is the primary technique of choice for tomato, cucumber, and pepper rising. Organic ingredients, such as composted milled pine bark (Pokorny, 1979) and coconut fiber (Morgan, 1999b), which have an environmental benefit over perlite and rock wool (Spillane, 2002a) because they are biodegradable (Johnson, 200

Ib), are often used as the rooting medium. Morgan (2003e) explains the properties and uses of a broad variety of growing media (substrate) (rockwool and stonewool, vermiculite, perlite, coconut fibre, peat, composted bark, pea gravel and metal scrap, sand, expanded clay, sawdust, pumice, scoria, polyurethane growing slabs, rice hulls, spaghnum moss, and vermicast and compost). She then matches the substratum characteristics to a particular method of hydroponic production.

Selection of propagated substrates is based on properties suited to germination and growth of seedlings (Morgan 2003f; 2004c). Other factors will decide which substrate is best, such as seed size, drainage requirements and continued usage after germination. Rockwool is perhaps the most commonly used substrate for germination. Fine textured germination substrates (particle size) are peat, sand, perlite, vermiculite, sphagnum moss, and coconut fibre.

Gravel, scoria, and expanded clay are coarse-textured substrates. Combinations of these materials may be used to create a particular characteristic, such as retention of moisture, drainage rate and weight.

Nutrient Solution Formulations and Their Use

The hydroponic literature is packed with different formulations recommended for a particular crop or use. For example, Jones and Gibson (2003) found 19 articles related to the formulation and use of nutrient solutions and some 32 different nutrient solution formulas recommended for various crops in The Rising Edge magazine in issues published between 1989 and 2002. Crop requirement is a significant factor that would determine the need for a particular formulation or application method. For most cases, usage directions are sketchy, which will leave the reader uncertain about how to dispense the nutrient solution to the plant (the application frequency and volume are not specified, for example). In general, automated methods are used for dispensing the nutrient solution, such as the dosing devices defined by Smith (2001f) and Christian (2001).

Throughout this chapter, formulations for use with a particular crop and/or hydroponic growing technique that have appeared in the literature are given. All guidelines for the formulation should be reviewed carefully before they are approved and used. The author's experience has been that only a few formulations are appropriate for widespread use. The type of hydroponic growing system, the growing crop and the environmental conditions are influencing factors that would require modification of the formulation / use recommendation. Many who want to make their nutrient solution from scratch should find Musgrave's (2001) guidance helpful, covering the Law of Conversion, the Calculation of Elemental Percentages, and the Rest of

Conversion Theory.

Cultivar/Variety Availability and Selection

There are no crop cultivars / varieties known as best suited only for hydroponic production. Breeding and selection are based on the production of plants that are ideally adapted to a particular climate, such as day length and light intensity, or plant characteristics such as resistance to disease, drought and/or heat tolerance, fruit habit and fruit characteristics (Waterman, 1993–94, 1996b, 1997b). Much has been written about "genetically engineered" species, engineered to achieve a specific characteristic, a subject that has stirred significant debate and controversy (Baisden, 1994; Waterman, 1997). Most of the breeding research has centered on the most widely grown crops and those which would be rated as "high cash priced," like tomatoes.

Recently there has been interest in varieties of "heritage" (Male, 1999; Johnson, 1999), those with substantial history of recognition and use. But in some forms of growing systems, many varieties, like heritage, do not perform well, whether hydroponic or not. There is also a lack of unique tolerance to disease in many heritage plants, one of the main focuses in the introduction of new species. Additionally, much of the breeding work has centered on cultivar production where the greatest need is. For example, greenhouse tomato cultivar breeding and selection were for adaptation to low-light, low-temperature conditions, whereas cultivars that would have high-light, high-temperature tolerance were given little attention. Additionally, fruit quality in terms of physical appearance, colour, firmness to withstand rough handling, quality of storage, etc. are some of the qualities that are developed in the newly released cultivars. Cultivar / variety selection is a major decision facing the grower, where a misselection will result in poor plant output and low quality of fruit.

Grower Skill and Competence

As with any plant growing company, the grower's ability will indicate the difference between success and failure irrespective of the growing system's operational efficiency. Others attribute this to a green thumb skill that some people seem to have — the sense of knowing what to do and when the contributes to optimum production of the plants. The author has visited several greenhouses, so it doesn't take long to quickly determine the grower's abilities so ability to handle the crop and greenhouse facility just by looking around. Of example, only the crop's physical appearance, such as its freedom from infestations of insects and diseases, is a reasonable measure of growers' skills. Answers to questions such as "what was the timeliness of the cultural activities being applied? What is the general state, within and outside, of the greenhouse environment, its cleanliness, the quality and performance of heating, cooling and air distribution systems? "Providing additional detail. These are some of the measurable aspects that can be used to assess the grower's and the workers' competence. For example, Smith (2002a, b) gives advice on what an NFT tomato grower needs to do when the crop is in full production to sustain fruit yield, advice that can be extended to any evaluation of hydroponic growers. What were the impressions from past training? All can be learned under the tutelage of a professional teacher from practical experience and/or hands-on instruction.

The author's experience has been that most hydroponic growing device failures occur because of a combination of factors. I saw the fall of a hydroponic industry in the state of Georgia during the 1970s. It occurred because of two primary reasons, the poor design and inefficiencies of both the greenhouse and hydroponic growing system, and the lack of experience and technical expertise on the part of the growers needed to operate the green-house / hydroponic system successfully. At about the same time, I witnessed the performance of a small group of tomato-greenhouse growers in southeast Georgia who were educated and directed by an accomplished professional skilled individual. When that person left to take a different role, many of the growers he trained and led shut down their greenhouses, afraid that attempting to continue without his guidance would inevitably lead to failure.

Grower performance depends on several factors other than the individual's inherent skill. Getting professional expertise in all aspects of the through system will contribute significantly to the success. Nevertheless, the consequences of a poorly built greenhouse or hydroponic growing system can not be reversed by any amount of grower ability and professional guidance.

Home Gardener/Hobby Hydroponic Grower

Hydroponics presents a challenge that some have taken up to the home gardener and hobbyist. Most have developed their own hydroponic growing systems based on knowledge contained in and from the internet in books, manuals, and magazine posts. Smith (2001a, b, c, d), explains how to design and create your own hydroponic system in a four-part sequence. He says, "My hydroponic sequence of introductories delved into the basics of what makes hydroponics tick. We covered the quality of your water supply, the different types of systems and the hydroponic nutrients your plants need." "Hydroponics for the Rest of Us "is the title of an article discussing different hydroponic growing systems (passive — wick system and active — flood-and-drain, top feed, NFT) and their operating requirements. The two recommended for the home gardener are the hydroponic flood-and-drain and top feed systems because they "perfect for home design and construction without compromising durability and quality" (Van Patten, 1992). Additionally, Van Patten (1992) divides processes into two additional types, recovery or non-recovery (respectively recirculation or discard) of the nutrient solution.

Coene (1997) offers basic details on soilless gardening, focusing on media- and water-based crop systems, nutrient solutions, artificial lighting, and pest control, and then explains how to create a growing vessel with a drip system. Likewise, Creaser (1997) gives instructions for building a drip system growing tray which he used to grow a variety of vegetables and house plants.

Peckenpaugh (2002a) recognized the need for hobby growers to provide a reliable source of hydroponic techniques and procedures. He explains the design and operation of four hydroponic systems (NFT, floating raft, ebb-and-flow, and drip), the formulation and use of nutrient solutions, including organic, and discusses the most commonly grown crops (cucumber, lettuce, pepper, strawberry, and tomato) plus how to treat insects and diseases. For one who just wants to play with small growing systems, Peckenpaugh (2002a) explains hydroponic growing techniques that "can be built by anyone with the time and patience to go through the process." In his article, he explains three different growing systems, Passively Wicking Pot, Styrofoam Cooler Grower, and Dutch Pot Dripper, describing the materials required to create each system.

For those who want to create their own hydroponic growing system for drip irrigation, Peckenpaugh (2003b) lists the following items needed: growing container, drip irrigation lines, drip emitters, nutrient reservoir, submersible pump, nutrient return line, growing media (expanded clay), and timer. He notes that "drip irrigation approaches the height of growing complexity due to its highly economical use of water and precise application of nutrients to the root zone of the plant." Expanded clay is the growing medium because it "holds some moisture and nutrients for plant use after the irrigation process, but does not get soggy or too wet." Peckenpaugh (2003c) explains its performance in using its homemade hydroponic growing system in a follow-up report.

Alexander and Coene (1995–96) concentrated on certain hydroponic systems that would draw the cost-conscious grower who wouldn't want to make major equipment investments. A simple passive hydroponic system, described by Christensen (1994b), may be a good place to start one's initial hydroponic venture; it is a spin off of an earlier-described hydroponic noncirculating system (Christensen, 1994a). Roberto's latest book (2001) offers "a guide to building and running hydroponic indoor and outdoor gardens, providing comprehensive guidance and step-by-step plans." Resh (2003) has a book on hobby hydroponics "to provide the reader with knowledge on the fundamentals of hydroponics that can be applied to a small-scale or hobby system." Angus (1995–96) offers guidance on how to run a hydroculture device consisting of five basic parts — clay pellets, nutrients, water level indicator, insert pot culture, and outer container.

Both these papers and observations speak of the wide range of possibilities as well as through structures that those interested in experimenting with the hydroponic technique can use.

Outdoor Hydroponics

The type of the least studied hydroponics today is their ability for outdoor use. Although hydroponics is initially practiced outdoors (Eastwood, 1947; Schwarz, 2003), the majority of hydroponic growing systems in use today are located in greenhouses or other enclosures. The difficulty, when the growing vessel is enclosed, is to find a hydroponic growing device that is not greatly influenced by rainfall. The least applicable outdoor hydroponic approaches will be those systems that use the nutrient solution distribution strategy for the drip.

From their comprehensive knowledge and experience, Bradley and Tabares (2000 a, b, c, d) and Bradley (2003) explain how simpler hydroponic growing systems are being developed by those in developing countries not only to tackle hunger but also to build small business projects. Included are easy-to-follow guidelines and operating principles for increasing systems which would be of benefit to anyone interested in hydroponics starting.

The personal experience of Ray Schneider, an enthusiastic hobbyist who first started out indoors (Schneider, 1998) and then went outdoors (Schneider, 2000, 2002, 2003, 2004) with his hydroponic NFT system, is an example of the successes and pitfalls that might happen. An article by Schneider and Ericson (2001) explains Ericson's learning experiences, using 6-inch sewer pipes as the growing vessel to grow hydroponic lettuce, bell pepper, tomatoes, cabbage, parsley, and herbs. Christian (1997) describes an NFT lettuce-growing program based on what was done elsewhere and how crop safety systems were built and used to deal with severe weather events over time. Kinro (2003) explains how Larry Yamamoto turned a hobby into a hydroponic lettuce-growing career using a simple floating raft device in Honolulu, Hawaii.

In a system where a depth of nutrient solution is retained at the bottom of a watertight vessel (box or trough) the author has had good success developing hydroponically. The growing medium is either pure perlite or a 50/50 perlite mixture of composted milled pinebark. A detailed description of the basic operating principle for this method is available on the www. GroSystems.com web site.

CHAPTER TWO

Hydroponic Crops

In the crop portion given later in this chapter, instructions are provided in the greenhouse on the hydroponic procedures for those crops which are most commonly grown hydroponically (tomato, cucumber, pepper, lettuce, and strawberry). The author has also successfully grown these crops outdoors hydroponically so updates on my observations will be made. The author has had strong success in growing vegetable crops, green beans, okra, sweet corn, and melons (water and cantaloupe) hydroponically outdoors. Instructions are also included for growing certain crops.

There are many benefits of hydroponically growing outdoors; the primary ones are managing water and plant nutrient elements, and preventing soil-related challenges such as weeds, poor soil physical and chemical properties, disease, and poor soil moisture management. Frequent references to articles in the magazine The Growing Edge are made as many articles contain useful tips for the hydroponic grower, whether commercial or hobby grower. The geographical range for the included crops depends on the literature base for that crop.

Morgan (2000d) provides information on growing "Baby Veggies," which are "appealing because of their appearance and tender flavour, and are typical cultivars harvested in their immature stage." Snow peas, squash, pumpkin, potato, eggplant, tomato, hot and bell pepper are grown in NFT systems; while globe artichokes, carrots, onions, beets and corn are grown in medium hydroponic systems.

Factors for Success

In terms of process (ebb-and-flow, NFT, media systems plus drip irrigation), and control of the supply of water and nutrient solution (and its formulations) to a crop, there is no standard hydroponic technique applicable in every situation. A key aspect is the use of the hydroponic device, whether in a greenhouse with its broad variation in design and function, in a controlled room, or outdoors. The physical location of a greenhouse or outdoor site in terms of geographic location at a specific site and/or in regions with varying weather conditions (high and low temperatures, and high and low light intensity and duration) will determine what is needed to be effective.

The abundance of knowledge available on hydroponics can easily lead to wrong choices being made in the design of the that system and the operating procedures. A common mistake is to follow a that framework and/or collection of operating procedures that only apply to a given environmental situation. What would be expected under low temperature and light, for example, would not necessarily apply at high temperature and light. What would be expected for a crop under decreasing light, from summer to winter months, would not relate to that under may light conditions, for example, from winter to summer months, what will happen with a fall vs. spring crop.

The selection of crops and cultivars should be based on adaptability to the growing system and environmental conditions and the marketability of the harvested crops. A common mistake is to produce a crop that either meets or does not meet market requirements, and/or is not of sufficient quality to be approved by consumers. A grower may be very effective in growing a crop but may not be in a position to market it properly. As stated earlier, one of the reasons a group of greenhouse tomato growers in southeastern Georgia was successful was that each grower had their own local market, but in addition they were able to pool their surplus fruit that was taken to a centralized market in a large nearby town.

Grower's expertise and familiarity with a specific method of growing may not be easily transferable to an inexperienced grower. The author has visited growers whose performance may be directly linked to their innate capacity, a feeling (the phenomenon of green thumb) that guides what to do and when to do so. Being proactive is often better than reactive to changing crop conditions or growing method. It is especially true when dealing with infestations of insects and diseases, or when there are evolving environmental conditions that would alter the requirements of plants for water and nutrient elements, or when shade or increased light is required. Failure to predict severe weather events, such as sudden low or high air temperatures, snowfall, or high winds, can result in damage to the greenhouse structure and to the status of an enclosed crop.

It is important to rely on qualified experts for identification and advice when addressing plant nutrition and pest problems. Monitoring and periodic testing are necessary to ensure a nutritionally adequate maintenance of the crop. Using tracking tools such as yellow sticky boards may show the amount of populations of insects. Knowing the degree of tolerance for both disease species and insects will help to decide when control measures are required, as there is usually no complete absence of such pests.

Unfortunately, even in the hands of a professional grower, not even the best built growing systems and greenhouse structures can initially perform well. It can take a period of "shakedown" to make the total system function effectively, and the can crop to meet expectations. In one set of environmental conditions, what might work can not work in another. This was the experience of four farmers in the southeastern United States, who initially produced high-yielding and -quality fruit and then encountered low yield and quality in the years that followed (Jones and Gibson,

2001). It's the ability to locate a problem's root and then change it or fix it, which allows for performance and minimizes losses. Record keeping is important if a grower is to continue growing high-yielding, high-quality crops. There should be regular monitoring of the environmental conditions. It should also document the dates when major events happened, and the crop's changing status. Accurate records of yield plus assessments of the output are important. A greenhouse tomato grower kept detailed records of weekly fruit production and then compared those yields with the amount of weekly sunshine, data obtained from local weather reports. Two or three weeks before, the highest correlation observed between fruit yield and weekly sunshine was obtained, indicating that the impact of weather conditions did not appear in the crop until several weeks later. Additionally, if yields are compared with growing conditions daily and/or weekly, these data can be used to direct the grower when making future decisions (Nederhoff, 2001).

The author knew a grower who kept constant records of any occurrence occurring in his greenhouse, including the exact time he entered and left every day. Such logs given to be necessary when a successful litigation against the greenhouse and hydroponic growing system supplier was brought. The grower was able to demonstrate successfully to the court that what the supplier had claimed in his printed brochures and manuals — predicted yield based on specified inputs — proved not to be so.

Constance of growing conditions contributes to high yields and the production of high quality goods. Every element of the environment, such as the amount of radiation obtained, can not be precisely monitored or the constant cycle of atmospheric conditions in the greenhouse or outdoors can not be adequately monitored. For most greenhouses, the use of computer-driven control devices (Lubkeman, 1998, 1999; Nederhoff, 2001) will reduce the cycling of the air temperature, CO_2 content, humidity etc. Growth chamber studies have shown what effect accurate control of the aerial environment can have on plant growth and development. The greenhouse system must therefore be so configured to replicate what is possible in a growth chamber if it is to achieve and sustain the environmental conditions needed for high growth.

Cycling of the supply of water and nutrient elements is not easily managed for most widely used hydroponic growing systems. There are three things occurring as a nutrient solution is added into the through medium. Plant roots absorb water and nutrient elements at varying levels in the nutrient solution (Bugbee, 1995), water and non-absorbed nutrient elements begin to accumulate in the rooting medium (Jones and Gibson, 2002), and some of the added water and nutrient elements leach from the rooting vessel. The effect is a rooting environment that continually varies and can adversely affect plant development. This is one of the driving factors that those engaged in hydroponic system research and development are not addressing adequately. Geraldson (1963, 1982) dealt with this problem in his work on the impact of the quantity and balance of nutrient elements on the growth of staked tomatoes grown in the field. Jones and Gibson (2002) use this basic principle in their creation of the Aqua-Nutrient growing system and forms the basis for a commercial product called the "EarthBox."

Much remains to be known on how plants can be best grown hydroponically. No major breakthroughs have occurred over the last few decades. Over past years most of the hydroponic growing systems in use today have been built. How the future holds for new technologies is unclear, as few are engaged in hydroponic system technology method.

CHAPTER THREE

Tomato (Lycopersicon esculentum Mill)

"Tomato story is a tale of three continents: South America, Europe and North America." The European chapter started in the 1500s, when Spanish and Portuguese explorers brought back unusual vegetables, one of which was tomato, to their respective countries (Bennett, 1997). The tomato has its roots in Ecuador and Peru's small, dry, tropical coastal areas but its domestication occurred in Mexico where it was discovered and brought to Europe. It's said the word "tomato" comes from Mexico's Nahuati language. Tomato was introduced to the United States in the 1700s, and is a major dietary vegetable plus a part in many food items (Smith, 1994; Jones, 1999). In the United States, fresh tomato fruit intake per capita is 19.5 lbs (8.8 kg), and that amount is expected to rise, primarily due to the health benefits that arise when it is included in the daily diet. There has been a significant change from beefsteak to cluster tomatoes in tomato type; the former are 30-40 percent, the latter 60 percent. Less than 10 per cent of overall production is in forms of cherry, plum and bell.

In the Netherlands there are the largest acres of greenhouse – hydroponic tomato, followed by Spain and England. In the Western Hemisphere, production figures are difficult to obtain, with an estimated 460 hectares (1134 acres) in Canada, 864 hectares (2134 acres) in Mexico, and 310 hectares (766 acres) in the USA. In Mexico the acreage is rising rapidly. Colorado State has fast behind in the U.S. Some have indicated that the future potential could bring the total acreage of greenhouse tomato production to 7000 acres (2833 hectares) in the United States. Wide greenhouse facilities [> 20 acres (8 hectares)] are situated at high altitudes [5000 feet (1524 m)], with high light (minimum cloud cover) and cool nights prevailing. Equally essential requirements for the selection of sites are the readily accessible sources of high quality water and natural gas. Since greenhouse tomatoes are not a crop tracked by the United States Department / Agriculture Research Service (USDA / ARS), it is difficult to obtain statistical data on acreage, rates of production, types of fruits, etc.

Tomato is the world's most commonly grown hydroponic crop, cultivated mainly in environmentally managed greenhouses and less often in open-sided shelters. Initially, some type of hydroponic growing method was used as an ebb-and-flow (Fischer et al., 1990), but in recent years, the nutrient solution has been preferred to go through irrigation. The tomato plant is either rooted in pure perlite (Bauerle, 1984; Day, 1991), rockwool blocks and slabs (Van Patten, 1989, 1991a, b; Robinson, 2002; Smith, 2003c), or some other substrate, such as coconut fiber (Morgan, 1999b). Johnson

(2001b) compared the characteristics of rockwool versus coir as a increasing medium, finding that cocopeat has a high nutrient- and pH-buffer potential and is environmentally biodegradable. Handreck (1993) gives the cocopeat (often referred to as coir) properties for use in a soilless potting medium and Ma and Nickols (2004) provide guidance on detoxifying coir dust and coconut shell. Morgan (2003f) explains media-based increasing systems and media-free methods (expanded clay, scoria, pumice, sand, and gravel), such as NFT (Peckenpaugh, 2002; Smith, 2003a, b, c) and DFT (deep flow technique) (Alexander, 2003b) and aeroponics (see pages 142–143). Papadopoulos (1991) explains the growth of organic medium containers, rockwool slabs, and NFTs in different systems. Smith (2003c, d, e) explains the evolution of PTO (Percy Tregida Otahuhu) farmers, who first started growing tomatoes in the soil in 1949, in a sequence of three papers. The NFT and the drip irrigation rockwool slab systems are now growing tomato in 1.5 million square feet of greenhouses. Many of the major hydroponic tomato operations [> 20 acres (> 8 hectares)] grow in rockwool slabs because this substrate is commonly believed to have the best control of water and nutrient elements. Most of the technology that is emerging comes from the Dutch growers, who grow almost exclusively in rockwool.

In an environmentally con-trolled greenhouse, factors that affect tomato fruit production are:

1.   Light, its intensity and spectral characteristics, and the length of the day (optimum: 1400 fc illumines, 14 hours of photoperiod)

2. The level of carbon dioxide (CO_2) in the greenhouse, particularly within the plant canopy

3. Air and root temperatures (optimal day / night air temperature, roughly 86/77 F (30/25 C)

4. Relative humidity ambient (optimum 50 per

cent)

5. Infestations of the insects and diseases

6. Composition of the nutrient portion of the nutrient solution applied and rooting mean

7. Tomato plant nutrition status

8. Cultivar Features

9. Days to bloom 50, days to ripen 100 10. Grower's Management Ability (high)

The tomato plant goes through four phases from seeding to final harvest, seedling period (4 to 6 weeks), vegetative period (2 to 3 weeks), early fruiting stage of first flowers to first fruit (6 to 8 weeks), and mature fruiting stage of first harvest before plant removal. Just before removal of the plant, the growing point is removed to promote the accelerated growth of the fruit of those still remaining on the plant.

Transplant Seedlings

The seed quality will decide the germination

rate, which is expected to exceed 95%. If seed is placed, it should be at 32–40 as much as possible (0–4.4 as possible). Over-seeding at 15 to 25 per cent would usually ensure a sufficient number of transplant seedlings. The optimum seed germination temperature range is 72–75 F (22–24 C).

Tomato seeds can germinate at 70 F (21 C) in 8 to 11 days. Seed age is one of the important quality factors, and some growers do not consider seed if the date on the package suggests the seed is over 6 months old.

Tomato seeds are not seeded directly into a hydroponic growing medium, as in soil growing, but are seeded in germination cubes or trays of soilless medium to create a seedling that will then be transplanted into the hydroponic growing system. Leskovar and Cantliffe (1990), Vavrina and Orzolek (1993), Snyder (1995), Meyer (1998), Fauly (1998), and Morgan (2002c, 2004c) have provided seeding and seedling growing procedures that will produce transplants that will bear fruit early. The critical factors are temperature and light, as well as sufficient nutrition to ensure a hardy seedling grows. It is the so-called "hardening or conditioning" cycle which will decide how quickly seedlings adapt after transplantation to their new environment. Morgan (2003e) found that the number of flowers located on the first truss increases when seedlings are grown at low temperatures [53–57 uF (12–14 uF)]. After transplantation the seedling character can decide the initial plant growth and the timing and location of the first cluster. Morgan (2002a) indicates that the trans-planting period is when the young plant is about to bloom, and then the first fruit is expected to grow under good growing conditions in around 7 to 10 days. The author has found that transplantation of seedlings shortly after the first "actual" leaves usually leads to best initial plant growth and early setting of the first fruit truss under high light and temperature.

Grafting

Seedlings grown to establish a double-steme plant or grafting onto a rootstock to increase plant vigor is becoming an increasingly common practice. Grafting on 17- to 18-day-old plants is performed at the seedling point. A good graft requires considerable skill; hence this is not a activity recommended for most growers to perform.

Crop scheduling

A two-crop system is used to avoid low-light months, and a single-crop system to avoid high-temperature months, depending on the light and temperature conditions. In the two-crop system, for instance in the northern hemisphere, a fall crop is planted in August and finishes in December, followed by a summer crop planted in March and finished in June or July. The crop is planted in September for the single-crop method, and finished in June. With additional lighting during low-light months, and shade during high-temperature months, changes can be made in either cropping method in plant scheduling.

Growing Containers and Medium

The most widely used tool for tomato growing is slabs of rockwool. The second most commonly used would be perlite in either bags or BATO buckets. Growers have also used a number of other substrates (cocopeat, composted milled pinebark, expanded clay, pumice, sand, gravel, or mixtures of these substances created to produce different physical and chemical properties) put in containers of varying depths and physical size. Morgan (2003f), describes the physical and chemical properties of these through media. The number of plants per sheet, container, or bucket will depend upon the configuration of the crop spacing. The medium volume in either bags or buckets will dictate irrigation frequency; the smaller the medium volume, the more often irrigation is needed.

The Japanese Top Graft Method

The scion (variety) and the rootstock are cut off at an angle of 45 and the scion is put directly on top of the rootstock with this method. They're maintained with a silicon grafting film.

Grafting shall contain the following actions:

1. Rootstock Seeding

2. Variety Seeding

3. Prerequisites

4. Cruising

5. Merger

6. Potting and chopping

1. Seeding the rootstock

Seed the rootstock, Beaufort in rockwool plugs at 240 cells per tray according to DRS recommendations about 5 to 10 days before the variety.

The seedlings are to be picked because of the uneven emergence. Currently this happens in the third true leaf stage (after 18 days). The selected seedlings are put at only 120 cells per tray in 240-cell trays (this is too hard to graft a complete tray). Selection is made every four to five days. The first time about 100 plants are usually produced per tray.

Keep this in mind for the number of plants needed within one time span.

Experienced plant breeders have a 95 percent success rate.

To make them thicker and more durable (18 to 20 C), selected rootstock seedlings should be held at a lower temperature.

In the event that another rootstock (i.e., PG3) is used for a more uniform germination, the flats that be seeded at 120 per tray immediately. For this reason special seeding equipment is available.

2. Seeding the Variety

Sowing as per regular guidelines.

Graft some 17 or 18 days later.

3. Grafting P reparations must be performed in an environment with no direct sunlight.

Create plastic tent, approximately 30 cm high. We prefer transparent plastic. The film has got to have enough energy. A white film can be used under the high light conditions. However, transparent plastic is preferred, and a retractable screen or Styrofoam sheets will minimize the intense sunlight.

Desinfect the palms, for example, with Virkon.

Razor blades: Do use new blades, and sometimes replace them.

Climate: temperature: 21 to 22 ° C; relative humidity (RH) inside the tent should be around 95% (wet floor or plant misting as well as within the plastic tent).

No smoking (virus) during the grafting.

Make sure the rockwool plug is extremely wet, EC 2 to 3 mS. 4. Grafting Technique Cut the rootstock at an angle of 45 with a razor blade. Depending on the conditions this can be achieved either above or below the cotyledons. Cut under the seed leaves when light and dry, to prevent sucker growth from the rootstock. When it is dark, make the cut above the cotyledons to take advantage of the extra photosynthesis. Set the clip for the grafting.

Cut off at an angle the range. (Suggestion: if hot or low RH, briefly place the scion in a tray with clean or sterile water) Place the scion in the clip to ensure good contact with the rootstock (i.e., air between the two parts may fail).

Remark:

1. It is preferred to cut at an angle (45) over a straight cut because the surface of the fusion is greater and the probability of success is higher.

2. The ideal situation is to cut both the rootstock and the above-cotyledon variety.

3. Cut the rootstock no more than 2 cm above the rockwool base. When greater, there is a chance that the graft may fall over; when smaller, the variety will root into the media.

4. If the variety has grown too quickly, cutting it higher (even as high as the true 2nd or 3rd leaf) is advisable.

Immediately put the grafted plants within the plastic tunnel. The optimal temperature for fusion is 21 to 22 C. Under sunny conditions, the mean temperature is 28 to 29 C.

5. Fusion

Avoiding direct sunlight on the plants and

maintaining a uniform climate is important. If it is sunny, shading will be necessary until the plants are hardened.

The most popular technique is to keep the tent closed for three days and to check on the fourth day whether the graft can survive. The plants are not to wane. When this occurs, mist the plants gently (don't use warm water).

Ventilate a little on fifth day. Making a small gap is preferred, and checking the condition of the plants every hour. If they wilt, spray the plants gently with clean water and cover the tent once more. The difference can be made again in the evening, or the next morning. Make the distance bigger on day 6, if the plants can handle it and remove the plastic on day 7 (preferably morning or evening).

6. Potting and spacing

The usual plant raising procedures can be

followed after day 7. It is advised to transplant into a rockwool block from 9 to 10 days after grafting (when the rootstock and variety have firmly joined in). (If the grafting clips were silicone, removal is not required.) The normal rockwool slab is 36 in. (91 cm) 6 "tall. Broad (15 cm), and 3 in. (7.6 cm) wide, 0.375 in.3 (0.0106 m3) volume; A typical perlite grow bag contains 1-1/3 ft3 of perlite (0.037 m3); the bag is 44 in. (111 cm) 8 "tall. Broad (20 cm), and 6 in. (15 cm) Tall. The BATO Bucket volume is 0.57 ft3 (0.02 m 3). Jensen (1997) recorded growing six tomato plants at a thirty-fifteen by 7.5 cm; each plant had a rooting volume of 2438 cm3 and needed 30 times daily irrigation. He also indicated that tomatoes were being successfully grown at the University of Arizona in a rooting volume of 956 cm3, although continuous irrigation during the day was necessary. The rooting medium's design and scale is determined mainly by economics, using as little average as possible to reduce initial expense and disposal requirements.

The author has developed tomato plants into fruiting bottles containing perlite in 20 oz (591 mL) beverage in which the nutrient solution is continuously supplied to maintain a 1-in. (2.5-cm) solution depth on bottle foundation.

The root mass was collected from a number of perlite-containing BATO buckets after 6 months of commercial tomato production at three greenhouses located in the southeastern United States. The author found that much of the root mass was surfacing around the outer edge of the perlite mass with few roots in the middle where the two nutrient solution delivery drip emitters were installed. This indicated that during much of the growing period, the repeated applications of the nutrient solution necessary to supply the plants with the water needed kept the center of the perlite mass anaerobic and therefore not an suitable area for active root growth. It may have been one reason for the decrease in plant growth and fruit production as the season progressed (Jones and Gibson, 2001).

There has been no thorough investigation into the impact of root size, development, and function on tomato plant development and fruit production when regular irrigation is required to meet high transpiration demands. In field soil conditions but not hydroponically to the same degree, what effect root physical restriction has on plant growth has been studied. If the plant can be sufficiently supplied with water, a relatively limited amount of root will satisfy the demand if there are no constraints in the rooting medium, such as high or low temperature, low O_2, and high EC. This has been demonstrated by the author in experiments performed in 20 oz (591 mL) beverage bottles; vigorous growth of tomato plants remained turgid under high atmospheric conditions. However, when the atmospheric demand is high, plant wilting is not uncommon, indicating insufficient absorption and transport of water from the roots to the transpiring leaves. Under those conditions, solutions would be possible to reduce atmospheric demand by shading and/or misting. The minimum root surface needed for a mature, active growing, and fruiting tomato plant is not known under ideal rooting conditions. Even under the best of conditions, the minimum that fluctuate with time as it is not possible to hold the rooting medium at the ideal condition continuously. So much needs to be investigated.

Plant Spacing

The region occupied by a plant is determined by spacing up the field. The region each plant occupies typically affects fruit yield per plant, as high plant densities normally result in lower fruit yield per plant. The light intensity decides what plant spacing is best for optimum yield. During the flowering and fruiting period, the greater the light intensity, the closer plants can be lined up. Canada, Mirza, and Younes (1977) suggest 2.7 plants per square meter in Alberta. Morgan (2003e) recommends a typical 2.5-plant spacing per square meter. New Zealand PTO growers use a plant density of 2.2 m2 per plant (Smith, 2003e). In a Canadian textbook, Papadopoulos (1991) recommends optimum room per plant as 0.35 to 0.40 m2, with a spacing of 31.5 in. in-row. (80 cm), the same as between rows in a double row arrangement, 3.9 ft (1.2 m) between two rows. Resh (1995) spaces plants in the row at 30 in. in a rockwool slab growing system under low light conditions. 18 to 20 in. (75 cm). (45 to 50 cm) between plants, corresponding to 6 ft2 (0.6 m2) per line. With improved lighting conditions the spacing is 3.0 ft2 (0.3 m2) per square foot. The rows are spaced 16 to 20 in. in a double row configuration. (40 to 50 cm) apart and spaced 12 to 14 inches in lines. (30-36 inches). The author spaces plants in the row in the southern latitudes, and at 18 in between double rows. (45 cm) across double rows, 3.0 to 3.5 ft (0.9 to 1.06 m). Wittwer and Honma (1979) gave 3.5 to 4.5 ft2 (0.32 to 0.41 m2) per plant as the optimum spacing.

Now, Mississippi space plants are greenhouse tomato growers in a setup to get 4 to 5 ft2 per plant, with 3 to 4 plants in 2-ft3 laid-flat perlite bags, and 2 plants per 5 to 7.5 gallon upright perlite-filled bags.

It is clear that the arrangement of plants and the number of plants per area are parameters which were not standardized. Many configurations may be used, such as single- and double-row setups, with often defined inter-row space to provide ample workspace. The greenhouse's physical design can be such that in order to fit in a certain number of rows a narrowing of the inter-row space is required.

Cultural Plant Practices Training the plant up a support chain, prompt removal of leaf axial suckers and vegetative stems from the fruiting truss, leaf pruning, flower pollination, fruit thinning on the truss and lowering of the growing plant are important daily activities for productive fruit development (Smith, 2001e). Both of these activities seek to hold the plant in a high fruit-productive state (Smith, 2002a). Depending on the cultivar and characteristics of the plant, the degree and timing of fruit truss thinning (removing small slow-developing fruit) and removal of leaves below the fruit trusses (generally, leaves below the lower fruit truss contribute little to the fruit growing above) can differ. A "single truss, single cluster" approach developed by the Rutgers University Cook College of Agriculture is being tested in a specific experiment, by restricting the tomato plant to one main stem and one fruit cluster. The hydroponic ebb-and-flow method is used, with the tomato plant grown in a cube of 3 inches of rockwool. Harvestable fruit is obtainable within 90 days of transplantation (Simon, 2003).

Environmental Conditions

The tomato plant is sensitive to both low and high air temperatures and to the strength of radiating radiation. The optimum daily temperature range for tomatoes is between 70 and 82 F (21 and 28 C), night time air temperature is between 62 and 64 F (17 to 18 C). Papadopoulos (1991) refers to acceptable minimum air temperatures with light conditions, a minimum night temperature of 64 F (18 C), a minimum daytime temperature of 70 F (21 C) and a minimum night temperature of 62,6 F (17 C), a minimum daytime temperature of 66 F (19 C) at low light. No fruit collection occurs at mean air temperatures above 86 F (30 C). Although air temperature is critical to best plant growth and set fruit, it is the temperature of the leaf that is equally or even more important. For example, if the air temperature around the plant is above that required, air movement over the surfaces of the plant's leaves and normal transpiration (water loss from plant tissues, typically through the stomata) will keep the plant "cold," and therefore in an active growing and fruit setting state. The author has found a lower temperature between air and leaf temperature as much as 10 degrees Fahrenheit as determined by infrared reflectance when the plants are actively transpiring in a moving environment. An average air push of 3.2 feet per second (1 meter per second) through the plant canopy is recommended. Air movement through the canopy will actively keep the plants transpiring, resulting in sustained photosynthetic activity (Srivastava and Kumar, 1995). The maximum relative humidity varies from 60 to 70%.

Harssema (1977) found the optimum root temperature to be between 60 and 86 u-F (20 and 30 u-C); plant growth was drastically reduced at temperatures less than 60 u-F (20 u-C). In addition, the transpiration rate increased with root temperatures varying from 54 F (12 C) to 95 F (35 C) respectively. Root temperature has not had the same effect on plant growth and fruit development as air temperature, and thus root temperatures within range 60 to 86 AF (20 to 30 AF) may not have a major impact on plant growth and fruit production.

Jones and Gibson (2001) found that there will be a decrease in fruit set and yield in southern latitudes where there is more than 10,000 minutes of monthly sunshine. Under conditions of high light intensity, shading is normally needed to control the amount of light entering the greenhouse, light radiation which generates heat in turn. For polyethylene-covered greenhouses when the greenhouse temperature begins to reach 85 ° F (29 ° C), it is usually recommended that a 40% white shade material be pulled over the greenhouse, while 50% white shade material is recommended for high altitudes and high light intensity areas (see Figure 12.15). The ideal greenhouse design will be to have movable shade that can be pulled over the crop when the light conditions are extreme and can then be quickly removed when the light conditions are lower.

Tomato irradiance requirement as per Manrique (1993) is 13 Mj / m2/d. Papadopoulos and Pararajasingham (1997) record a low of 2,01 to 2,65 kg of fresh fruit weight harvested for every 100 Mj of solar radiation the crop receives. So the main factors restricting fruit yields are short days and low radiation fluxes in northern latitudes in the winter months. The efficacy of supplementary light in winter months to address low radiation flux is doubtful. Gain, if obtained, exists by increasing the light time instead of attempting to raise the light flux during daytime. Photon flux within the wavelength range of 400 to 700 nm [photosynthetically active radiation (PAR)] is the one used effectively in photosynthesis, with light measurements represented as photosynthetic photon density (PPFD) (Mplekas, 1989; Parker, 1994a, b).

Since tomato is a C3 plant (the first photosynthesis product is a three-C carbohydrate-containing product, see page 378), the rate of photosynthesis activity peaks at relatively low light intensities and is significantly sensitive to the CO_2 content of the air surrounding the plant. The intensity of photosynthetic activity can be increased under low light conditions when the air's CO_2 content is maintained at 1000 ppm (Slack, 1983). The value of the ambient atmospheric CO_2 ranges from 300 to 400 ppm. At normal CO_2 levels, individual leaves reach optimum assimilation rates at approximately one quarter of the available radiation from full summer sunlight, with some leaves actually absorbing 80 to 90 percent of the PPFD light incident.

When tomato plants enter the wire that supports the lines of the plant bond, the plant canopy becomes thick and no air movement occurs within the canopy unless air is introduced at the bottom of the canopy so that air passes through the canopy. Having air moving through the canopy has two major benefits, preserving the

CO2 content in ambient air (300 to 400 ppm) and increasing transpiration, which keeps the plant foliage cool. The author claims that the air movement up through the canopy of the plant often prevents white flies (Bemisia argentifolli Bellows and Perring) from landing easily on the plant foliage. Even with the use of high-velocity fans, it is very difficult to move air from above down into the plant canopy.

Tomato plants also greatly reduce their absorption of water as the root temperature decreases (Figure 11.20). Water use declines dramatically as the temperature of the rooting falls below 68 F (20 F) and above 86 F (30 F) (Tindall et al., 1990). For example, on days of high atmospheric demand, the tomato plant may wilt even if there is enough water available when the rooting medium is cool [less than 68/F (20/C)] or the EC is high (> 4 dS / m). The effect of the moisture stress is slow plant growth and poor fruit collection, as well as increased fruit blossom-end rot (BER) incidence.

Additionally, there is a substantial drop in nutrient absorption as root temperature decreases. Tindall et al. (1990) found that since the rooting temperature ranged from 50 ° F (10 ° C) to 104 ° F (40 ° C), tomato plants greatly affected the absorption of the major elements and micronutrients. The influence on temperature did not affect all major elements and ions as well as K, Ca, and NO3--while P, Mg, and NH4 + were not. Fe, Mn, and Zn were substantially impacted for the micronutrients.

Water Requirement

Within this book earlier plant water needs were addressed. Some of the most important decisions to be taken by a grower is when to drink, and how much. The majority of hydroponic delivery systems are set on a time clock such that the nutrient solution and/or water is added to the rooting medium at regular intervals, whether the plant needs it or not. A system that involves radiation measuring devices and a computer program designed to estimate water requirements based on past atmospheric demand plus plant size and fruiting status (Rudder-Hasenohr, 2000). Some of the common fruit disorders, such as BER and cracking, are caused either by under- or overwatering.

The tendency is usually to overwater, which can contribute to anaerobic conditions in the growing medium. Carefully extracting the perlite from a number of BATO buckets that had been growing tomato plants for more than six months, the author found that most of the roots surrounded the perlite layer. In almost every case, the center where the nutrient solution was being applied to the surface through the drippers had little if any roots present. Examining the roots' location in the rooting medium, therefore, will say a lot about the current conditions of aeration.

There are fewer flowers per truss at low water

supply, low fruit set and an increased occurrence of BER. Deficient plant production, later flowering, fewer flowers and lower collection of fruits occur under high water supply (overwatering). With regular water supply shifts the frequency of fruit cracking increases. Because of the concern of the PTO growers about water availability and the likelihood that the root zone could be periodically too dry, they moved from NFT to a rising rockwool substrates network (Smith, 2003c).

The water required by the plant is supplied via the nutrient solution in most of the hydroponic nutrient solution supply systems. Therefore carrying water to the plant roots requires all of the elements in the nutrient solution, elements that the plant does not require. Many of the high levels of nutrients contained in plants can be due to overfertilization from unneeded elements that are added only when water is needed. The ideal design would be to have two supply systems, one for the nutrient solution and the other for water, so it can be applied alone when only water is required.

Under normal growing conditions, water use varies from 17 oz (500 mL) to 0.26 gal (1 L) per day while the tomato plant is flowering and setting fruit. Ward (1964) developed that tomato plants use water to be 3 gal (11.3 L) per plant per week. It is estimated that it will take 4 gal (15 L) of water to produce 1 lb (0.45 kg) of the harvested fruit. The exact amount of water required during flowering and the fruit setting and growth cycle will depend on the rate of transpiration of the plant, which is associated with the degree of incoming radiation; the higher the radiant energy, the greater the water use. In addition, the level of air movement within the plant canopy, as well as the high air temperature and low relative humidity, would also increase water use.

The author and Wignarajah (1995) claim that aeroponics is the "ideal" hydroponic growing system where "nutrients are constantly flowing down the roots that have access to ready supply O2." Unfortunately, aeroponics is not an economically viable process for growing crops such as tomatoes, cucumbers and peppers.

Flower Pollination

Naturally occurring insects are typically necessary for adequate pollination of tomato flowers in the field. Nonetheless, in the greenhouse either hand flowers pollination at midday every other day when the relative humidity is minimal using an electric hand pollinator and/or the introduction of bumblebees (Bombus spp.) into the greenhouse is needed. The size and number of required hives would depend on the number of greenhouse plants. There will be approximately four flowers in bloom on each plant during flowering and fruiting. Insufficient numbers of bumblebees can be found to properly pollinate all the emerging flowers as well as too many bumblebees, which can result in flower damage and fruit loss. Those who provide bumblebees will advise on the size and/or number of hives needed based on plant number and greenhouse configuration. The environmental conditions of the greenhouse will decide the effectiveness of the bumblebees, and how long a hive will live. Bumblebee operation can be impacted by the use of pesticides and supplemental lighting as well as other greenhouse conditions. Information can be collected from bumblebee suppliers regarding certain conditions which will impact bee operation.

Some pollination happens as wind pushes the plants, or the flowering truss is pushed by physically shaking the plant. These methods of pollination, however, are typically not adequate to ensure complete pollination, resulting in incorrect fruit in turn.

Such unpollinated flowers should abort the fruiting truss. Certain factors such as low light levels, high air temperature, plant wilting, and nutritional insufficiencies (such as high N) can also cause flower failure. However, emerging flowers may abort when plants bear a heavy fruit load, and when environmental conditions are less than ideal.

When hand pollination is performed using a vibrator, enough force is required to dislodge the pollen. When the pollen is mature, while the truss stem is vibrating, a yellow pollen cloud can be seen dropping from the flower. Care must be taken to ensure the vibrator does not come into contact with small fruit that grows. If contact is made a scar may appear as it matures on the fruit.

Fruit Development and Yield

To understand how fruit grows, one needs to have an understanding of the relationship between source and sink. Through the photosynthesis cycle, carbohydrates (source) are developed and divided into one of three plant parts (sinks) to help plant roots, expand new plant growth, and develop fruit. The partitioning is affected by the growing conditions surrounding the plant, such as light intensity and length, air temperature and CO2 content and plant water status, as well as how the crop is handled (sucking, removal of leaves, removal of flowers and fruits, etc.). Maximum carbohydrate transport to the fruit occurs when the air temperature is between 73 and 75 F (23 and 24 C) and when plants are sufficiently supplied with water and plant nutrient elements required to sustain adequacy. Fruit will ripen from 40 to 75 days after pollination; the time taken represents an association between factors dictated by cultivars and growing conditions. So long as there is a fruit left on the plant, its size will continue to grow. Fruit that is in the shade will ripen more slowly, so it will be larger at harvest than fruit that is in the sun. The weight of the fruit will depend on the quality of its water; the higher its quality, the greater its weight. Ninety-five per cent is water for tomato plants.

There is no clear term for reporting fruit yield weight, so that simple comparisons can be made between the different production methods. Fruit yield (weight) can be expressed on an area-based basis, on a per-plant yield over a specified time span, or total yield over a defined growing season for a production unit (i.e., whole greenhouse). For example, either 63 kg / m2, 1.0 to 1.5 lbs of fruit per plant per week during the fruiting / harvest time, or a total of 40 to 50 pounds per plant for the entire growing season (about 7 months) will be described as a "healthy" fruit yield. The author assumes a "high" fruit yield will be a sustained amount of 1.5 to 2.0 lb per plant per week of production. Smith (2003b) stated that "the Dutch have historically been the trend-setters for greenhouse cropping and research dedication has some Dutch growers now yielding around 70 kg / m2 (around 50 lb / plant)." Another factor not usually known is the actual number of fruits harvested. Moreover, most fruit yield data contain only "marketable" fruit — fruit that is defect free and appropriate in size. The main determinant of fruit yield is the number and weight of fruits. Fruit weight (size) is determined mainly by cultivar but may be influenced by growing conditions such as air temperature [higher than 72 ° F (22 ° C) increases fruit maturation levels] and shading, whether naturally shaded by the leaves of the plant or artificially shaded, which slows fruit maturation levels. Toping (removal of the growing point of the plant), a procedure used before the end of the growing season, may improve the rate of fruit growth and ripening.

The author performed a hydroponic greenhouse tomato experiment in which fruit yields were exceptionally high, primarily due to the weight of individual fruit, weights in the 12 to 14 oz (340 to 397 g) range when fruit weights were supposed to be 8 to 10 oz (227 to 283 g). One aspect determining yield (based on weight of the fruit) is the fruit's water content.

Those factors which would increase fruit's water weight would increase fruit yield. Ripe tomato fruit should be stored in a relative humidity environment of 85 to 90 percent at temperatures between 40 and 50 F (4.4 and 10 half C) and if so stored fruit quality can be preserved for 6 to 12 days. Fruit should not be stored with fruit which produces ethylene, such as apple or banana.

Fruit Quality and Flavor

Fruit quality is determined by many factors, grade (U.S. No. 1, U.S. No. 2, U.S. No. 3, color rating (green, breakers, turning, yellow, light red, red, defect rating (damage, extreme damage, very serious damage), and similar varietal characteristics (Jones, 1999). Fruit can be separated by size (diameter) and/or weight and marketability for "beefsteak" style varieties [free from blemishes, i.e. cracking (Peet, 1992), catfacing, misshapen, puffiness, BER, sunscald, green shoulders, russetting, more scarring, fracturing, and blotchy maturing. Morgan (2001e) discusses possible causes of fruit anomalies and then describes steps that can be taken to reduce them. Color uniformity, strength of color, and firmness are also factors which will decide the marketability of tomato fruit. At the "split" point, fruit can be harvested when the fruit initially turns from dark green to light green and then allows it to mature naturally or be handled with ethylene gas to speed up the process of maturation. Color production pictures of 10 to 100 percent ripe tomato fruit can be found opposite the Wittwer and Honama (1969) inside title page of the novel. Fruit from tomatoes picked when green never matures naturally.

While flavor is not a calculated fruit identification factor, high flavor (organoleptic properties) sensed by the customer can lead to repeated sales for known origin labeled fruit. There are two measured factors associated with the "strong" taste, a 5.8 to 6.2 dS / m EC fruit, and a 4.8 to 5.0 BRIX level. Flavour can be a subjective aspect because not everyone can taste the same thing. In general, fruit containing high acidity and sugar is usually called "flavourful." Much of the flavor in the tomato fruit occurs in the portion of the gel. Hence, the fruit's gel-to-wall ratio can affect flavour.

High flavor comes from two components of the fruit, sugar content (glucose and fructose), and volatile organic compound amounts. Forty-six per cent of the fruit's dry weight is sugar, 12 per cent organic acids, 8 per cent minerals, and the other organic compounds that remain. The longer the fruit is left on the vine, the stronger its taste will be. The cooler the temperature of the air, particularly the temperature at night, the greater the flavor of the fruit. In general, stressed plants grow higher-flavored fruit; this is the rationale behind the standard practice of raising the nutrient solution EC to approximately 4 dS / m or adding NaCl to the nutrient solution at a concentration of 35 ppm in solution during the fruiting cycle. A varietal aspect is present, as some varieties produce more flavorful fruit than others. Small-fruit varieties (cherry) tend to contain more flavor than large-fruited (beefsteak) varieties usually do.

Two other factors that will affect quality measured by consumers are skin toughness and firmness of the fruit, factors that offer a certain "mouth feel."

Plant Nutrition

The tomato plant is known as a plant requiring high nutrient elements. Primary nutrient elements of importance for this crop are N, P, Mg, and Zn. Among the micronutrients, the tomato plant has high Fe and Cu requirements, and modest B, Mn, and Mo requirements. Excess N is more likely to occur than its deficiency; excess results in abortion of the blossom, reduction of the collection of fruits and vegetative stimulation over reproductive development. Plant characteristics that suggest excess N are dark green foliage, robust plant growth, rapid growth and sucker production, and the presence of vegetative stems on fruit trusses. Plant N amount considered excessive varies with plant growth stage and environmental conditions. Moreno et al. (2003), for example, found that cultivars less effective in their use of N yielded higher fruit yields than those more effective. They also observed that total N in the leaf tissue declined with time; the average content was around 4.50 percent during the vegetative stage and then decreased to 3.00 percent during the fruiting phase at a gradually decreasing plateau rate. Though in agreement with Wilcox (personal contact), Ward (1964), and Reisenauer (1983), the 3.00 percent N amount is substantially less than what was recorded by some (Jones, 1999) as the optimum during fruiting. During this same time,

Moreno et al. (2003) observed a decrease in leaf K (4.00 to 2.00%), Mg (0.90 to 0.70%), and S (0.32 to 0.20%), while P (0.75 to 0.95%) and Ca (2.90 to 3.10%) increased. Mason and Wilcox (1982) say that the NO3-N content of the petiole of mature leaves (> 14,500 ppm is excess) is a better measure of the tomato plant's N-status than total N of the entire crop.

While fruit quality is commonly thought to be closely correlated with elements K and B, little attention has been paid to N as an significant factor affecting the quality of the fruit. The author assumes that controlling the K supply to the plant does not affect the quality of the fruits unless the plant's N status is preserved at the lower end of the sufficiency range (3.0 to 3.5 per cent). Light intensity can also play a significant role in the tomato plant's Nutrition, requiring higher N levels under low light conditions, and lower N levels under high light conditions.

Blossom-end rot (BER) is a symptom of Ca

deficiency due to inadequate Ca entering the blossom end of the fruit that grows. However, if there is no other stress condition that results in BER-affected fruit a serious Ca deficiency must occur. More often than not, BER occurs primarily as a response to plant stress, usually stress with moisture and/or low transpiration rate. Calcium moves through the plant's xylem conductive tissue, and if that movement is slowed down by impaired water uptake and/or movement through the plant, then Ca movement up the plant is also impaired, particularly movement into fruit growth. Furthermore, ample Ca in the rooting medium, while necessary, does not guarantee liberty from BER occurrence. As reported by Taylor and Locascio (2004), "BER is linked to several factors, including: high salinity, high concentration of Mg, NH4 and or K, inadequate production of xylem tissue, rapid growth rate, unfavorable moisture relationships (high, low or fluctuating), low soluble medium Ca, high temperature, and high and low transpiration." Calcium is not readily absorbed through the leaves into the plant, and then transferred through the fruit epidermis to the vascular tissue for transportation across the plant.

There is also a balance between the major cations, K, Ca, and Mg, and if these components are out of balance with each other, then it can impede Ca uptake and movement. The author observed BER-affected fruits when symptoms of Mg-deficiency on the visual leaf were present. The presence of NH4 in the nutrient solution will significantly increase the incidence of BER if it is greater than 10 per cent (Hartman et al., 1986).

Excess phosphorus is more likely to occur than its deficiency, and its excess (greater than 1.00 percent of the dry weight) may result in Zn deficiency in recently mature leaves (Jones, 1998a).

Not only can the source of Fe affect its

absorption but it can also have a major effect on the plant. For example, the type of Fe in chelate ethylenediaminetetrateacetic acid (EDTA) is not recommended as EDTA is toxic to the plant (Rengel 2002). Fe's form of chelate diethylenetriaminepentaacetic acid (DTPA) is the approved chelated form since toxicity to DTPA is assumed to be absent. Rengel (2002) found that Fe-EDTA's inclusion in a nutrient solution resulted in a decreased absorption and translocation of the Cu and Zn micronutrients within the plant. It is not known if chelated Fe's DTPA shape would have the same impact on both of these micronutrients. They used other chelated forms of Fe, HEEDTA, NTA, and EDDHA, but to a lesser degree than either EDTA or DTPA. Several inorganic forms of Fe, such as iron ferrous sulfate, $FeSO_4 \cdot 7H_2O$; iron ferric sulfate, $Fe_2(SO_4)_3$; ferric chloride, $FeCl_3 \cdot 6H_2O$; and iron ammonium sulfate, $FeSO_4(NH_4)_2SO_4 \cdot 6H_2O$, have been found suitable as sources of Fe in nutrient solution formulations.

In tomato leaf samples submitted for review and interpretation the author has frequently found low contents of Cu and Zn. The questions to be answered are, "do these low levels represent an insufficient amount of Cu and Zn in the nutrient solution," or "is this a factor related to cultivar adsorption ability, or is it the nutrient solution effect of Fe chelate on Cu and Zn adsorption? "The effect of the presence of chelate in the nutrient solution would be my best guess. I have found in earlier experiments that if the source of Fe was an inorganic one, low content of Cu and Zn leaf was not frequently observed.

The plant's nutrient-element status is essential for normal vigorous growth and sustained fruit setting and production under varying environmental conditions. For example, the best plant output is obtained under high radiation (bright long sunny days combined with high transpiration rates) when the plant's nutrient content for the major elements, primarily N, P, and K, is at the minimum concentration required for their sufficiency. The best plant output occurs under low radiation (short and/or cloudy days with low transpiration rates) when the plant's nutrient element content for these same major elements is at the mid- or higher end of the concentration range needed for their sufficiency.

The absorption levels for the critical nutrient elements are not all the same as Halbrooks and Wilcox (1980) have found. For elements P, K, and Mn and for ions NO3- and NH4 +, active uptake occurs; moderate uptake for elements Mg, S, Fe, Zn, Cu, and Mo; and passive uptake for elements Ca and B (Bugbee, 1995). Actively transpiring plants can quickly pick up the NO3– and K+ ions from the solution surrounding the roots, resulting in high N and K levels in the plant, which in turn contributes to imbalances between these and other components. Therefore there is a need to change the composition of the nutrient solution to prevent imbalances between the components.

Morgan (2003d) found that the concentration of the major elements in a nutrient solution would change over a period of 40 days, as the plant blooms and sets fruit. The K concentration, for example, decreased from 750 to 200 ppm, while Ca increased from 500 to 700 ppm, and Mg increased from 125 to 200 ppm, respectively. To account for these changes, Morgan (2003b) suggested that the nutrient stock solution be formulated in such a way as set out in Table 11.11 to account for those changes.

The plant's nutrient element content can be controlled by regular sampling (every 2 to 3 weeks) and analysis. The right sample is an end leaf from a newly mature crop. Physical signs of plants suspected of being due to a deficiency of the nutrient factor should be checked through plant analysis. The book by Roorda van Eysinga and Smilde (1981) gives color pictures of the visual symptoms of nutrient disorders in tomatoes. Bould et al. (1984) describes visual impairment symptoms for the elements Ca, B, Cu, Fe, Zn, and Mo in the novel. In a review article, Jones (2000) explains the tomato plant's nutritional characteristics, and how visual plant appearance and elemental leaf content can be interpreted as a means of ensuring adequate nutrient element. Insufficiencies of visual nutrient components in tomatoes are in video form (Jones, 1993c).

Varieties (Cultivars) Several varieties are available for outdoor production; the plant types are determined (the plant may end its growth by producing a flowering truss) or indeterminate (the plant continues to produce a vegetable stem), and the fruiting characteristics differ greatly in size, color and shape. The following favorite tomatoes were identified in a survey conducted by Organic Gardening magazine (vol. 50, issue 4, page 4, July / August 2003): Beefsteak — 37 percent, Cherry — 27 percent,

Slicer — 20 percent, and Plum — 15 percent.

Bennett (1997) lists 'home garden favorite tomatoes,' including 19 cherry tomato varieties, 59 medium size tomato varieties (average fruit weight from 2 to 10 ounces), 27 big tomato varieties (average fruit weight 12 ounces), 15 paste tomato varieties and 22 rare tomato varieties.

Heirloom varieties are of increasing interest (Male, 1999), but many of these varieties are susceptible to various diseases and may lack adaptability to climate stress (Johnson, 1999).

Varieties used in earlier periods were beefsteak styles for greenhouse production, such as "Tropic" and "Jumbo;" while varieties produced by Dutch researchers such as "Trust," "Play," "Hunt," or "Blitz" have been used in more recent times. Most of the so-called beefsteak cultivars originally grew but today cluster tomatoes are becoming the variety of choice due to their special market presentation. It is estimated that about 60 percent of all today grown greenhouse tomatoes are a cluster, and that percentage can continue to increase.

CHAPTER FOUR

The Hydroponic Greenhouse

The analysis is strictly restricted to greenhouse systems of less than 0.5 acres (0.2 hectares) in scale, with particular regard to a 3000 to 3600 ft2 (279 to 334 m2) stand-alone greenhouse or multi-bay units consisting of two to five stand-alone unit bays. There are large greenhouse facilities, consisting of 20-acre (8-hectare) units which may be situated in a two to six-unit complex. Large greenhouse complexes are somewhat similar to what could be called the "single-owner / operator" greenhouse, but there are significant differences beyond the scope of this analysis in terms of design and operational requirements.

The size unit(s) best fits for the single owner / operator should be determined by the economic and market conditions. Pending the verdict, what follows in this chapter shall apply.

There is nothing unique about hydroponics that would significantly alter the basic structure or operating characteristics of a greenhouse, features that can be found in Aldrich and Bartok's books (1994), Hanan (1998), Nelson (2002), Betyes (2003), and Taylor (2003), as well as in Goldberg (1985) and Beytes (2003) papers. The basic requirements are focused on which plants to cultivate (Nelson, 2002). The only thing that may be different inside the greenhouse would rely on the method of hydroponic production, be it in containers, field beds or troughs, or in pits placed on the greenhouse floor or benches. Specialized equipment can also be required for supplying plants with the nutrient solution and water. For example, an ebb-and-flow or NFT system may need a particular means to store and distribute the nutrient solution for a drip irrigation system. For a hydroponic ebb-and-flow system the nutrient solution tank is usually placed below the level of the growing beds in the field. For example, the size of tanks that contain nutrient elements may be deciding their position inside or outside the greenhouse.

Placement can also require other means of temperature control to ensure the temperature of the nutrient solution supplied to the rooting medium is equivalent or equal to that of the greenhouse air temperature. If collected, the effluent flow from containers, slabs, and troughs would require a collection, pumping, and storage system, but if discharged it would require a floor design to manage such drainage. Such nutrient solution discharges now come under water quality legislation, requiring storage and treatment before discharge (Johnson, 2002c). The NRAES-56 publication (Anon., 1996) covers guidelines for effective management of nutrient solutions, concepts of root zone management, water quality and distribution, and related topics that that affect the operation of a hydroponic greenhouse;

Savage (1985b, 1989) has two publications on the financial aspects of building and maintaining a hydroponic greenhouse.

Greenhouse Defined

The early term for defining a greenhouse was "hothouse," a term that is not widely used today. The hothouse is described as "a greenhouse maintained for the cultivation of tropical plants at high temperatures," in the Merriam-Webster Dictionary. This concept derives from the fact that a greenhouse will collect solar radiant energy which heats up the interior. Jensen and Malter (1995) described a greenhouse as 'a framed or inflated structure, covered by a transparent or translucent material which allows optimum light transmission for plant production and is protected from adverse climatic conditions.' Hanan (1998) states that 'greenhouses are a means of overcoming climate adversity using a free source of energy, the sun.' The term 'glasshouse' is a European phrase for a building that is artificially heated for growing plants' (Gough, 1993). Beytes (2003a) describes three basic greenhouse designs, one-bay free-standing as low-cost entry into the greenhouse market (Thompson, 2003); multi-bay gutter-connected as the most effective practical greenhouse (Grosser, 2003), yet lacking in flexibility; and withdraw.

Location Factors

In earlier times (before 1970), greenhouses dedicated to vegetable production were located near major population centres, but with the ability to shift producing rapidly from one area of the country to another, and even from neighboring countries, site selection could be based on factors other than market closeness. Jensen (1997) announced the collapse of the greenhouse vegetable industry that once existed in the central United States around major population centers. He notes that "today ... light is considered the most important factor in greenhouse vegetable production, rather than being located near a population center." Some may refute this statement, as many single-operator greenhouse vegetable growers are successfully growing and selling their produce on local markets, which are often large population centers.

The location and placement of the greenhouse can decide how well the enclosed crop performs other than economic considerations. Resh (1995) lists the specifications of the following site: 1. Full east, south, west exposure to windbreaked sunlight on north

2. Level region or one conveniently levable

3. Strong internal drainage, with minimum 1-in./h percolation rate.

4 Have natural gas, three-phase electricity, telephone and water of good quality which can supply at least half a gallon of water per plant per day

5. On a good road near a wholesale business center and greenhouse retail market if you want to sell retail 6. Near to the residence for ease of greenhouse testing during weather extremes

7. Greenhouses focused north-south with rows even north-south

8. A area that has a maximum sunlight content of

9. Not situated in an environment of extremely strong winds

In addition, the greenhouse should be positioned so that the greenhouse is not shaded by features in the immediate region. Wind exposure may have a major effect on the heating and cooling requirements; thus, it may be highly beneficial to have a windbreak. Placement on hill tops in rolling terrain will expose the greenhouse to uncontrollable winds and cold air runoff, fog and polluted air in the valleys.

It is important to determine what exists upwind, even several miles away, to avoid either deposition of dust on the greenhouse or the possible intake of substances that would cause harm to the enclosed crop. To position the greenhouse in an actively cropped field, it is important to know what crops are being grown and what chemicals are being applied to those crops. Many crops, such as soybeans, are ideal hosts for insects; insects can be brought into the greenhouse via the ventilation system, thereby contributing to the requirements for pest control. Herbicides and other chemicals that are spread aerially to surrounding fields and fruit crops can be transported into the ventilation system by flowing into the greenhouse. Getting a windbreak may mitigate the accumulation of suspended material that can collect on the surface of the greenhouse or the immediate area. The author visited a massive greenhouse complex, which was situated in an remote area within miles with little human activity. Selecting such an isolated location would mitigate what the surrounding human activity could bring into the structures.

Therefore, the immediate environment surrounding a greenhouse must be kept as sterile as possible, with the minimal interference from activities that may churn up airborne particles, such as having adjacent service buildings that carry vehicle traffic close to greenhouse entrances.

At one time the author was responsible at different locations for a sequence of field plots of study. The yield results were significantly different from those obtained at the other sites at one spot, a site east of a highly traveled highway. It wasn't until I calculated the volume of ammonia (NH_3) above the plots in the atmosphere that I understood why the results of yields at this site were always greater. The NH_3 coming from truck and automotive exhaust was deposited as ammonium-nitrogen (NH_4-N) on this field plot, which added enough N to the crops being grown on those plots to significantly influence yield.

The author was curious as to why a large greenhouse operator selected a certain region in the southeast for the foliage plant production. In addition to the availability of an educated work force and a suitable living environment, the specific location was decided based on long-term weather records which showed a high number of cloudless days for that environment during the year. A similar greenhouse location in upstate New York was chosen because for that specific site, the regular light conditions based on long-term sunshine data records were higher than those for the surrounding area.

Basic Structural Design

A greenhouse's structural design is important because the size and spacing of framing material will influence the degree of light shadowing, whereas other types of structural materials may serve as thermal accumulators, contributing either desirable or undesired heat to the greenhouse atmosphere. The ability to withstand wind and snow charges will dictate the strength required for the structure, which is a major factor in certain areas. A common mistake in greenhouse design is to underestimate the effect of extreme climatic events (wind, hail, and snow) on the structural integrity and protection of the interior. Treated wood, galvanized steel, aluminum tubing, and PVC tubing are widely used structural materials.

Greenhouse systems range from a loose covering over the top of the crop (Wells, 1996), with or without mobile side curtains built to shield plants from rain or from the extremes of outside temperatures, to a fairly airtight system for precise monitoring of the internal climate. Polyethylene film-covered greenhouses usually have end walls of solid, clean plastic (polycarbonate). The typical style for polyethylene film-covered shelters is Quonset (mark for prefabricated shelter set on the base of bolted steel trusses and semicircular arching-roof).

A single-bay commercial greenhouse structure can differ dramatically in physical size: length from 90 to 130 ft (27.4 to 39.6 m), width from 24 to 40 ft (7.3 to 12 m), and height from 8 to more than 12 ft (2.4 to 1.6 m) to the gutter.

The greenhouse height can have a direct impact on the heating and cooling systems' ability to maintain a consistent air temperature within the structure. The greater the volume of air to be conditioned tends to minimize significant changes in temperature, humidity, and concentration of CO_2 in the interior air.

Freestanding greenhouses and gout connected have different design requirements. Gutter-connected greenhouses give flexibility in construction and use of space but add additional criteria for managing the interior. Wide open areas present challenges to disease and insect control as well as special equipment in the system to maintain consistent atmospheric conditions.

The design of the entrances and the placing of screen coverings over air vents and other openings will determine how well insect and disease organisms can be prevented from entering the greenhouse (Jacobsen, 2003). The entry of the main door into the greenhouse will be installed in a door-shaped addition, close to entrances to most business buildings. Workers will change clothes before entering the device, step into a disinfectant room, etc., and then enter the greenhouse without injecting a blast of air into the greenhouse if the ventilation fans are working.

How well the various parts of the greenhouse fit together will decide how "tigh" the structure is going to be, a good feature to keep out unwanted air and insects, but if it is too "tightened," irregular air pressure from inside or outside will lead to cracks and deterioration of joined pieces.

For greenhouses covered with glass or rigid plastic, these structures either have mobile vent panels on the rigid side, or large mobile vents that can open the entire greenhouse roof. The typical design for most plastic film-covered greenhouses is to place an exhaust fan(s) at one end of the greenhouse, and an adjustable opening, with or without a cooling pad, at the other end so that air can be pulled through the greenhouse duration. Air baffles can be mounted in the gable at various locations, so that air pulled through the greenhouse by an exhaust fan(s) is regularly guided downward, ensuring that air mixes across the entire depth and duration of the greenhouse. A very efficient way to ventilate a greenhouse is to position the ventilation fans and cooling pads around the greenhouse length on opposite sides, so that air is drawn across the shortest distance.

Unfortunately, it is so built that few greenhouses are.

Flooring In the greenhouse a variety of materials can be used as flooring; concrete is the best choice, and compacted soil or sand is the least suitable choice. The walkways may be concrete for initial cost considerations, while the crop rows may consist of sand or gravel, or similar materials. In order to act as a buffer, the crop rows and, if the whole floor consists of such materials other than concrete, the plastic ground cover should be placed over the crop rows or the whole floor. Crop waste, a source of disease and other problems, which falls on an open floor can not be cleaned up unless the floor is strong. The lack of flooring firmness will cause user issues, affect the flow of foot traffic in the greenhouse as well as interfere with the floor drainage system. With a smooth and solid flooring material in place, the entire greenhouse floor pays dividends in concrete to keep the floor clean and clear of waste. The greenhouse floor will have a slope of I to 2 per cent.

Glazing Materials Glazing refers simply to the type of material that covers or that is attached to the greenhouse structure. Another word used in the glazing literature is cladding (which, according to the Merriam-Webster dictionary, covers or overlays); Glass, polyethylene foil (high or low density, linear low density), ethylene vinyl acetate, and coex-truded films are the widely used glazing products. Fiberglass was used widely at one time, but its flammability has restricted its use almost completely today.

Coene (1995) lists five major considerations when choosing the green-house coverage:

1. Integrity of materials in direct sun, without losing clarity

2. Lifetime Guaranteed

3. Resistance to the Fire

4. Photosynthetic radiation transmission (PAR);

5. Assets on energy efficiency

Another function is the diffusion of light which passes through the cover. Light diffusion can more uniformly disperse light in the greenhouse, resulting in "a more even distribution of light without specified shadows" (Coene, 1995). Fiberglass has a high diffusion property as well as structural strength; for these purposes it was used as a glazing medium in wide use at one time.

Some types of coverings do not transmit all the wavelengths of light that reach their surface equally, thereby filtering the light and altering its spectral characteristics (Morgan 2003a). The characteristics of different types of glazing materials including glass, polyethylene film, polycarbonate, fiberglass, and acrylic are discussed in the Beytes (2003a) edited book. Both of these materials have different transmission properties which will have a direct effect on greenhouse radiation input and output.

Cost, durability, and external environmental factors (i.e., wind, snow load, hail resistance etc.) can decide the selection of which glazing material is best. The so-called "greenhouse effect" is a phenomenon owing to a wavelength change. Radiation leaving the greenhouse contributes heat to the interior as radiation reflected back from the interior surfaces is longer than that leaving the greenhouse and is therefore stored as heat inside the greenhouse.

The effect of light filtering and diffusion on the color and design of the plant was demonstrated to the author in a greenhouse tomato experiment performed in two greenhouses a few miles apart. One greenhouse had fiberglass insulation, the other glass. The plants in the glass-covered house were dull green in color and had long internodes, while those in the fiberglass-covered house were dark green with short internodes in colour. Interestingly, there were only minor variations in fruit yield, but the tomato plants in the greenhouse covered with glass needed more regular adjustment due to their longer internodes.

Heating and Cooling

The specifications for heating and cooling will differ according to the location, form of structure, and crop to be grown (Anon., 1994; Ball, 2003; Rearden, 2003; Morgan, 2003a, b). Typically speaking, it is easier to oversize these systems to ensure that the atmosphere within is easy to manage. The location of ventilation fans, cooling pads, and heating equipment can dictate how well the temperature and moisture inside air can be managed. Air movement up through the plant canopy is favoured for certain crops, such as tomatoes and cucumbers. Floor heating can be beneficial to a crop especially in cooler climatic areas, keeping the rooting medium at or near the greenhouse ambient air temperature. The warming of the nutrient solution / water to that of the current greenhouse air temperature, or even 4 to 5 degrees F above ambient air temperature

(Smith, 2002b), would decrease the potential for plant wilting due to decreased water absorption. The rate of plant roots absorption of water is correlated with temperature, decreasing as temperature decreases (Nielson, 1974; Harssema, 1977).

Heating

There are two methods mainly available for heating the greenhouse atmosphere, forced hot air or radiant heat. The most widely used is either a natural gas or propane-fired jet fan heater which is mounted on the ventilation fan end in the greenhouse gable (Figure 12.8). Heated air is forced through a wide plastic-holed tube gable-placed which runs the entire length of the greenhouse (Figure 12.9). The heated air is circulated through the holes in the pipes, the discharge force being sufficient to drive heated air into the cavity of the greenhouse. In the fossil fuel combustion contributes heat to the atmosphere. The moisture can condense as the ambient temperature cools the underlying greenhouse system, leaving the walls and internal structures wet, including the plants, which is highly unwelcome.

The other form of heating is by passing either boiler-generated hot water or steam through pipes that are installed at ground level down the sides of the greenhouse, and in some cases, pipes are installed between crop rows. This sort of heating system is called "hydronic heating;" through radiation from the heated pipes, it allows even heating of the greenhouse atmosphere. The greenhouse and canopy atmospheres are kept dry with hydronic heating, as hot air flows through the plant canopy into the gable from floor-level pipes. The moisture-laden air can then be expelled from the greenhouse using a small gable-placed ventilator.

Three processes result in heat loss from the greenhouse: conduction (heat loss from solid materials), convection (removal of heat from air currents), and radiation (heat loss from the glazing layer by short or long wavelength radiation). Additionally, heat loss can occur through the absorption of cool air and hot air loss through the greenhouse cracks and openings. A winter weather temperature can be estimated, based on the average of the coldest days of the year. For very cold environments, either outside or at the base of the gable as well as on the sides of the greenhouse, the use of thermal blankets can greatly minimize back radiation at night, or when the greenhouse is exposed to cold winds. Figure 12.10 (Bartok, 2000) shows the winter design temperature chart for estimating heat loss in greenhouses located in the continental United States.

Morgan (2001b) explains the greenhouse architecture and operating procedures required to mitigate the impact on plant growth and greenhouse functions of low temperatures. She focuses on the selection of glazing materials, the design of heating systems, and the procedures for air distribution, which can have a major impact on the maintenance of the interior environment within parameters necessary to maintain plant production. Double layers separated by continuously applied air reduce heat loss by both conduction and back radiation for plastic polyethylene film-covered greenhouses. Likewise, polycarbonate twinwall panels are widely used as end walls but they can be used as side walls as well as glazing material; the double-walled material is more energy-efficient than single-walled panels.

Floor heating can be beneficial in certain climatic regions. It is done by either putting on the surface or in the greenhouse floor itself hot water – heated pipes or electrical heating cables. A thermal barrier is installed beneath the greenhouse floor for the most effective floor heating effect.

The range of temperature in which plant enzymes are active ranges from 50 to 104 F

(10–40 C). For most greenhouse-grown plants, the optimum air temperature ranges from 55 F (13 C) to 77 F (25 C). At low temperatures, plants may display signs of a P deficiency, a violet pigmentation of the new leaves, and below, some cases, symptoms of Fe deficiency — symptoms that will disappear when the greenhouse air temperature is brought into the normal range for best growth. Low air and medium temperatures can lead to pathogen development (especially Botrytus), as well as reduced water and/or nutrient solution uptake at the root.

For heating greenhouses alternative sources of both fuel and heat were used. For example, waste oil (Anon., 1977b) and methane emitted from a landfill (Simon, 2003) were used as sources of fuel, and hot water condensate from a nearby steam-powered electrical plant was used to heat a greenhouse (Peckenpaugh, 2004b). Kleemann (1996) explains how wind-powered generators can be used to provide a greenhouse with electric power.

Johnson (2003) describes a specific hot water storage system in which water is heated by a gas-fired boiler during the day to 200 F (93 C) and CO2 produced by combustion is introduced into the greenhouse after passing through an exhaust gas separator (see CO2 enhancement section). At night the greenhouse is heated with the accumulated hot water.

During the winter months (December through February in the northern hemisphere, June through August in the southern hemisphere) in some climatic regions where light intensity is small and regular average daytime air temperatures are typically less than 32 µF (0 ° C), there is little attempt to develop under these conditions.

Cooling

It should be recalled that a greenhouse, often referred to as a "hothouse," is a very powerful solar collector (thermal accumulator), probably ideal in cool / cold low-light climatic conditions but an undesirable function in high-light warm / hot climatic conditions (Morgan 2001a; Jones and Gibson, 2001). The so-called "greenhouse effect" is due to the trapping as heat of incoming radiation in the greenhouse — heat that is not readily re-radiated through the glazing material back out. Furthermore, incoming radiation that reaches the objects in the greenhouse serves as heat sinks, contributing significantly to the heat load that can either be advantageous or detrimental to regulating the interior. Buntyn-Maples (1994–95) talks about "Greenhouse Growing — Southern Style, where plants face adverse 40 F (4 ° C) temperature days and even colder nights without indoor supplementary heating or greenhouse solar power." Many growers in the southern regions do not grow due to high temperatures in the mid-summer months (June – August). Jones and Gibson (2001) linked poor growth of tomatoes and fruit yield to the amount of radiation (measured as sunlight minutes per month) entering greenhouses in southeastern United States. We found that the output of tomato plants was negatively affected by months of more than 10,000 minutes of cumulative sunlight.

The natural way to extract warm / hot air from the greenhouse can be as easy as raising side curtains or opening ventilation vents at the roof ridge line if the greenhouse is so built. For structures without these features, cooling is obtained primarily through the ventilation fans dragging outside air into the greenhouse (Ball, 2003). The fans are mounted at one end of the greenhouse or along its sides, and the openings at the opposite end or side draw air in. Those openings can be fitted with a cooling pad that is kept damp by passing or moving through water. The efficacy of the cooling pad in reducing the temperature of incoming air will depend on the relative humidity of the outside air; the higher the humidity, the less the temperature of the air will decrease. It is possible to measure the configuration and effectiveness of cooling pads based on the pad size and the amount of air drawn through the pad (Short, 2003). Any gallon of water evaporated through a cooling pad from the passage of air will consume 8100 BTUs of heat energy.

The author claims the greenhouse is much more effective in cooling the interior than dragging air through the longest distance. Few greenhouses are therefore equipped with side ventilation systems. Depending on the weather conditions, 60 air changes an hour could be required on days of high light intensity to maintain optimal air temperature inside the greenhouse by bringing cooler air in from outside.

Opening the greenhouse to outside air that flows into or out of the greenhouse would enable the entry of insects, disease species and other pests. Screens of different mesh sizes (below 500 micron mesh recommended for insect blocking) are required to minimize the entry. If the primary cooling system is via a cooling pad, it can require a wide screened plenum to allow sufficient air to move through (Jacobsen, 2003).

Shade cloth placed over the greenhouse will decrease the amount of incident radiation passing through the glazing or, when placed at the bottom of the roof gable above the canopy of the plant, decrease the air temperature in the greenhouse or canopy of the plant respectively. When to shade and the amount of shade depends on which crop is being grown and on the radiation intensity being provided. For example, shade should be applied to tomatoes when the daytime greenhouse temperature reaches 85 ° F (29 ° C), and shade should be applied to lettuce and herbs when the daytime greenhouse temperature is greater than 80 ° F to 82 ° F (26.6 ° C to 27.7 ° C).

Shade cloth pulled over the top of the greenhouse is not easily put or removed as shown in Figure 12.15, which offers little flexibility for sporadic use. More recently, at the gable base, the greenhouses are equipped with shade cloth inside the greenhouse that can be drawn over a crop or fairly quickly pulled back. The ability to position and eliminate shade can have a major benefit in controlling the amount of radiation that impacts the crop, and in maintaining better control of the interior.

The degree of radiation control can vary according to the shade material's mesh characteristics. Normally, white shade material over a polyethylene-covered greenhouse is recommended for 40%, whereas white shade material for high altitudes and high light intensity light areas should be recommended for 50%. Glass-covered greenhouses have been whitewashed in the past to reduce incoming radiation, a practice that is not in general use today.

Misting is another way to cool down the plant

canopy. It is often used both to cool down and to provide protection from the effect of high light intensity to newly rooted cuttings or emerging seedlings. The disadvantages of this technique are the potential for the development of disease when there is a cool and humid environment, as well as the requirements for high pressure pumps, fine nozzles and water free of suspended particles (Beytes, 2003). For certain environments the amount of radiation entering the greenhouse can be greatly decreased by misting or running water over the greenhouse roof.

Nyun (1997) has built a unique side wall lath shading method "squiggly cut" for use with greenhouses of a hobby kind.

Morgan (2001a) discusses those procedures necessary to minimize the effects on greenhouse operations of high temperatures. The temperature effect on the enclosed greenhouse crop varies with species, and how well the cooling system functions. The basic influencing factors are related to greenhouse design, such as increased roof heights and roof vent inclusion, and the use of fans and aspiration screens to move cool air through the greenhouse at different heights.

For most greenhouses, the impact of uneven cooling on a crop between the cooling pad and the exhaust fan can be easily seen if the transporting air is pulled at a significant distance [> 50 ft (15 m)] and there is no air mixing in between. The difference in air temperature may be as much as 10 degrees Fahrenheit from the end of the cooling pad to the end of the ventilation ventilator. For example, if tomato is the crop and the height of the canopy is at the support wire, the cooled air that is pulled through the cooling pad would appear to move over the canopy top. Such a condition can have a significant effect on plant growth and fruit yield. The solution would be to have a pad-ventilation cross-flow fan system (pulling air through the greenhouse rather than down its length), and/or moving air from its base through the canopy. If the cooling pad has an inner door closure, the closure should be hanged at the top so that air coming out of the pad is directed at the base of the canopy of the plant.

The plant cools itself by transpiration, the removal of water vapor from the surfaces of the leaves, close to the effect evaporating suddenness has on the body. The effectiveness of this refrigeration method includes continuous air movement over the surfaces of the leaf. Inadequate O2 and/or water in the rooting medium and low temperature can impair the movement of water into the plant roots (Nielsen, 1974; Harssema, 1977). The nutrient solution's increasing electrical conductivity (EC) will also diminish water uptake (see page 106). Under either of these restricting conditions for water uptake, the plant may wane when there are high conditions for atmospheric demand. Low air temperature and stagnant air will slow down the upward movement of water in the plant's conductive tissue (xylem), thereby reducing the rate of water loss from leaf surfaces. Both conditions will affect photosynthesis efficiency, thereby slowing plant production, resulting in lower fruit yields in turn. Adequate air flow through the plant canopy is therefore important, particularly for certain crops, such as tomatoes and cucumbers. This can best be accomplished by installing air conditioning at the bottom of the canopy of the plant.

Air Movement

Air movement throughout the greenhouse, and particularly within the plant canopy, can have a significant effect on plant performance. In an enclosed greenhouse, air movement created by the operation of heating and/or cooling equipment may not be sufficient to thoroughly mix the air in the entire greenhouse (Short, 2003). Even the placement of fans in the greenhouse gable directing air into the plant canopy can be ineffective. With a dense plant canopy created by tomato and cucumber plants, for example, it is very difficult to push air into the canopy, as the canopy acts like a "box," and air movement directed at the canopy either passes over the top or glances off of it. Therefore the air within the canopy has characteristics (temperature, humidity, CO2 content) of its own which can be quite different than those of the air surrounding the canopy. The only way that sufficient air movement can be obtained is by the introduction of moving air from the base of the canopy so that air is constantly moving up through the canopy. This air may be conditioned, that is, either heated or cooled. If no air is being brought into the greenhouse from outside, it is very important that the entire mass of air within the structure be constantly mixed as plant growth and function can be impaired by standing in still air.

Plant Support System

For tomato, cucumber, and pepper greenhouse production, a plant support system must be installed. The system usually consists of a strand of strong wire stretched over the plant row with hanging string attached to the wire at each plant location. The plant is tied to the string. Various systems have been devised to ensure that sufficient string is present at each plant location to provide for lowering and tying over a full season of plant growth. The attachment of the support wire to a structural greenhouse member is not recommended since the plant weight on a support wire can be several tons. Most greenhouse structural members are not able to hold such weight. The support wire should be attached to sturdy-set stanchions placed about every 30 ft (9 m) down the plant row, or the stanchion can be placed in the middle of a double row with a cross piece at the top to hold each support wire in place.

Supplemental Lighting

There are two key reasons for providing additional light: photosynthetic, the use of light sources to provide part or all of the necessary for normal plant growth, and photoperiodic, needed to regulate flowering and plant shape (Yoemans, 1991; Sherrard, 2003). The amount of light required for photosynthesis for many plants ranges from 100 to 1000 times that needed for photoperiod lighting. If used for any use, the cost of additional lighting will be either equal to or less than the financial gain achieved from its use. Supplementary lighting to prolong the hours of daylight could be the only permissible use for most crops for photosynthetic benefit. Enhanced lighting to improve light intensity during daylight hours is highly doubtful as regards the substantial gain calculated by improved yield and product quality. For example, the light level in the greenhouse for sustaining tomato and lettuce growth ranges from 800-1200-foot candles. The light requirement of plants varies considerably, and supplementary lighting will help those plants that are highly light sensitive. Parker (1994a) gave some of the crops commonly grown in the green-house the light requirements.

In a two-part article, Parker (1994a, b), describes the characteristics of light, its nature, intensity, and spectrum, and its effect on plants. In the second Parker (1994b) paper, the spectral distribution for different lamps (standard fluorescent, mercury vapor, metal halide, and high pressure sodium) is discussed. A light source's suitability for supplementation depends on its spectral distribution (how close the light emitted mimics of the sunlight) and its intensity. The running expense and life expectancy of lamps are likewise significant considerations. For certain cases, the best spectral coverage for optimum plant impact can be provided by a combination of lamp types, such as incandescent and fluorescent, mounted over a crop. Combination lamps are available today to provide a broad spectrum of emitted light. Some lamps produce considerable heat, which can either be an advantage as a heat source or allow dissipation of the unnecessary heat, which adds to their operating costs. Supple-mental light also has a "drying effect" which keeps the plant foliage dry during periods of low light.

The type of lamp, its emission strength and spectrum (long and short wavelength distribution), the use of reflectors, a combination of types of lamps, and the positioning Light quality (spectral distribution) and strength are important considerations when selecting the type of lamp. Van Patten (1998), concentrating on high-intensity discharge (HID), metal halide (MH), and high-pressure-sodium (HPS) lamps, defines the types of lamps available for plant use. Metal halide lamps emit a complete, close spectrum to that of natural sunlight. One type of HID lamp is the sulfur lamp, light that comes from a hot gas or plasma within a transparent shell.

Those seeking a thorough analysis of the effect of light, both quantity and quality, including the effect of supplementary lighting techniques on plant growth and development, will find considerable value in Mplekas' (1989) post. Mplekas (1989) notes "the the need for a scientific approach to horticultural lighting in order to increase plant production and boost the economic return on an increasingly competitive market combines to emphasize the importance of electric lights as a horticultural control tool to the commercial grower."

Carbon Dioxide Enrichment

Carbon dioxide (CO2) naturally occurs at between 300 and 400 parts per million (ppm) in the atmospheric atmosphere and is considered an important plant nutrient by some. Simply put, CO2 diffuses through open stomata of the chlorophyll-containing leaves of a live plant and, in the presence of light, is combined with a split water (H2O) molecule to form a carbohydrate; the whole process is called "photosynthesis" (see pages 14 and 383). Positive effects of CO2 enrichment have been documented on plant growth since the 1920s, but greenhouse CO2 enrichment was not put into action until the 1960s.

The atmospheric CO2 content in an enclosed greenhouse will decrease during the day due to photosynthetic activity (CO2 absorption) and increase at night as plants breathe (CO2 release); the change in concentration is as much as 150 ppm. This cycling of the CO2 content can be moderated by regular ventilation of greenhouse and air mixing within the plant canopy. The CO2 depletion rate is closely associated with the photosynthesis rate, with the depletion occurring rapidly within a few hours of daylight. The author was shocked when he found a 50 ppm decrease in CO2 content inside a canopy of a tomato plant just a few minutes after the greenhouse entered direct sunlight at dawn (Harper et al., 1979). Photosynthetic behavior of plants will reduce the CO2 content within the canopy of plants to between 200 and 250 ppm.

The photosynthetic rate is positively associated with the plant's CO2 concentration; the magnitude of this concentration effect varies with plant species (whether plants of C3 or C4, see pages 378–379) and light intensity (Carrathers, 1991–92). Therefore, the positive enhancement effect may be substantially enhanced if the CO2 concentration is three to four times that which is naturally present in the atmosphere, whereas photosynthesis can be halted when the CO2 concentration exceeds 200 ppm. Excessive concentrations of CO2 (2000 + ppm) can be harmful to plants, while concentrations of 5000 ppm can pose health hazards to those who work in such an environment (Morgan, 2003c).

Elber (1997) and Morgan (2003d) investigated

the impact of CO2 enhancement on plant growth for crops such as tomatoes, cucumbers, bell peppers, roses, lettuce and herbs, and ornamental and forage crops. The magnitude of the enhancement effect varies with crop species and is not always advantageous.

Slake (1983) found that all-day CO2 enrichment maximizes the growth of tomato plants and their fruit yield, but more importantly, maintaining the CO2 level within the plant canopy constant during the day to maintain plant growth and fruit yield. It should also be recalled that newly emerging leaves should have less stomata per leaf area with sustained high concentrations of CO2 (1000 ppm), and it is through the stomata that photo-synthesis takes place. Therefore, although the CO2 content of the atmosphere around the plant is high, due to the presence of fewer stomata on the leaves, the photosynthetic rate will go down. In addition, some observed a fairly large drop in photosynthetic response of plants to elevated CO2 over time, with initial increases ranging from 30 to 50 per cent and then falling to 5 to 15 per cent (Wolfe, 1995).

The light intensity and the CO2 content of the air surrounding the plant are also substantially related (Mpelkas, 1989). Gaastra (1962) also observed a significant relationship between the concentration of CO2, light intensity and temperature of the leaves, and the rate of photosynthesis in the cucumber. Increasing rising light intensity, due to either CO2 concentration and/or leaf temperature, the rate of photosynthesis was approaching a plateau. These plateau events will restrict the efficacy of CO2 enrichment with increasing environmental conditions and plant features.

Elber (1997) explains the different ways in which CO2 can be released into the greenhouse by either constant ventilation, the use of fuel-burning generators (which can also produce excessive heat and water vapour), or the use of bottled-gas emitters. If CO2 is produced using a combustion technique, care must be taken to ensure that there is complete combustion. Incomplete combustion will release greenhouse gasses, such as ethylene (C_2H_4) and carbon monoxide (CO), which will be harmful to plants as well as greenhouse workers, particularly if CO is released. Closed CO_2 generation and crop delivery loop systems have been developed for special applications, but need effective heating and cooling systems plus the ability to extract unnecessary combustion-generated released moisture.

Since CO_2 is heavier than air, it is usually added at the top of the canopy of the plant, and then spread through diffusion downwards. In tall green-houses (30 ft or more) with open roof vents, CO_2 can be added at the base of the canopy as it is then gradually transported from the base of the plant canopy to its top by the upward flowing air, thus improving photo-synthesis. If a greenhouse requires regular ventilation by bringing in outside air for cooling, the benefits of CO2 enrichment will be reduced, and the generation cost will surpass that gained from whatever increases in plant growth and fruit yield occur.

Johnson (2003) explains how a rose grower in a gas-fired boiler extracts CO2 from an exhaust gas separator that is then pumped into the greenhouse during the day from hot water production (200 F; 93 C F). The hot water collected at night is used to heat up the greenhouse. Likewise, for the introduction into their tomato greenhouse, the PTO growers produce CO2 from their natural gas heating system (Smith, 2003c).

Climatic Control

The interior greenhouse climate needs to be monitored and managed continuously to maintain the optimal environmental conditions for the crop being grown (Beytes, 2003b). The performance characteristics and cost of the sensors used to track the greenhouse environment differ considerably. Some greenhouse control systems are based on devices which track some factor, such as air temperature, and then enable either heating or cooling devices to bring the temperature back to the set range or point (Roberts, 1985; Gieling, 1985). The sensitivity of the measuring tool, the location in the greenhouse and its reaction time will often result in a wide-ranging cycling character of the interior environment which may not be best for the growing crop.

Major improvements in sensing devices have been made, leading to improved performance. Sensors coupled with computer-activated devices can "feel" a change and then trigger those devices required to maintain the atmosphere at the desired level, thus minimizing the greenhouse environment's cyclical character. Lubkeman (1998) stated that "computer technology helps bring better quality plants onto the market as it provides full control of the greenhouse environment." In his article, he explains devices for measuring temperature, relative humidity, air movement, CO2, lighting and light intensity, timers and master controllers, all necessary to provide the required controls to manage the greenhouse properly. Computer monitoring of greenhouse operations and management decisions was found to minimize material and labor costs, reductions that range from 15 to 83 per cent (Lubkeman, 1999). Johnson (2000a) notes that "Central computer control is certainly the direction greenhouse management is heading into the future; it has already proved to be the most efficient labor-saving method of today." Today, the greenhouse operator has several different control systems to choose from, and the decision as to which system would function best for greenhouse operations would require professional input. The 1994 Green-house Systems International Conference (Anon.,

1994) continuing contains papers relating to methods and procedures for managing the greenhouse climate in the interior.

For example, the installation of sensing devices outside the greenhouse for measuring air temperature, wind velocity, and light intensity will provide useful information to the greenhouse control system, thereby minimizing the impact of external conditions on the greenhouse climate.

Backup Systems

Sanitation warning systems should be standard equipment for informing off-site greenhouse managers and automatic backup equipment in any greenhouse. Failures are not always convenient; they typically do not occur even when workers are in the greenhouse or nearby so that appropriate action can be taken. Many crops were lost or severely damaged due to lack of electrical power or mechanical failures, as there were no quick-acting contingency measures in place. When high temperatures (both cold and hot) are present, it can take just a few hours of power or mechanical failure to seriously damage a crop. An electrical failure left under hydrostatic head pressure a hydroponic tomato grower to use urban water as he was unable to operate his water / nutrient solution delivery system as well as receive water from his reverse osmosis system. He had no backup electric generation system and had not stored enough treated water to meet the demand during the power failure period. Owing to the water stress and the water quality applied, no harm occurred in its plants. When treated water is required to create a nutrient solution and water plants, the amount of water should be enough in storage for several days to satisfy the demand. In terms of energy generation, it will be necessary, depending on the electrical demand, to compromise on what would be needed to withstand short power loss times. Having a greenhouse in an area where daily power outages occur wouldn't be a smart idea. The failure of heating and cooling systems presents a greater problem in terms of access to immediate service personnel and/or the availability of spare parts for rapid repair of a failed unit. It is critical that a contingency plan is in place for all potential failures, and that all greenhouse workers understand it.

Greenhouse design criteria for keeping insects and other pests out pose a problem in managing greenhouse entries as well as sanitation-conscious surrounding area management. On almost any item (clothing, shoes, equipment, containers, boxes, etc.) it is easy to carry disease species and insects into the greenhouse; thus, there is a need for strict sanitation procedures. Keeping greenhouse walkways and outer edges clean; prompt elimination of dead, diseased, and insect-infested plant tissue; and restriction of other operations (such as fruit sorting, measuring, packing, etc.), are some of the criteria that will keep the greenhouse free of damaging infestations. The type of greenhouse flooring and its ease of cleaning can have a major effect on the ability to prevent falling plant debris from being a source of disease and infestations of insects. Standing water on the greenhouse floor or moving water up through the flooring material may contribute significantly to the atmospheric humidity.

Some managers limit movement in and out of the greenhouse by making workers spend in the greenhouse all their working day. Removal of street wear and work in sanitized uniforms is not a uncommon custom. Having workers walk through a chemical footbath would sterilize boots before reaching the greenhouse. Managers also have tough nongreenhouse visitor policies. Both of these measures are intended to mitigate the potential for entry into the greenhouse of insects, disease species and other substances that could adversely affect the enclosed crop. The author was once a member of a group of research scientists who regularly visited tomato greenhouses in the Cleveland area, Ohio. We needed to pick our tour schedule carefully, because some greenhouse managers would not let us visit if we had already been in greenhouses where there was a reported disease, tobacco mosaic virus.

The inside of the greenhouse offers an perfect habitat for rising visitors, animals (mainly rodents) and insects. Their presence does not pose an immediate danger to the crop itself, but it may cause substantial harm to the greenhouse structure, as well as harm to electrical cables, piping and control equipment. We can also carry out into the greenhouse disease species, insects, and weed seeds.

www.ingramcontent.com/pod-product-compliance
Lightning Source LLC
Chambersburg PA
CBHW071625150726

48000CB00004B/1892